THE COMPLETE BOOK OF
FERNS

THE COMPLETE BOOK OF

FERNS

INDOORS ➤ OUTDOORS ➤ GROWING
CRAFTING ➤ HISTORY & LORE

MOBEE WEINSTEIN

COOL
SPRINGS
PRESS

First Published in 2020 by Cool Springs Press, an imprint of The Quarto Group, 100 Cummings Center, Suite 265-D, Beverly, MA 01915, USA.
T (978) 282-9590 F (978) 283-2742 QuartoKnows.com

Cool Springs Press titles are also available at discount for retail, wholesale, promotional, and bulk purchase. For details, contact the Special Sales Manager by email at specialsales@quarto.com or by mail at The Quarto Group, Attn: Special Sales Manager, 100 Cummings Center, Suite 265-D, Beverly, MA 01915, USA.

24 23 22 21 20   1 2 3 4 5

ISBN: 978-0-7603-6394-2

Digital edition published in 2020
eISBN: 978-0-7603-6395-9

LIBRARY OF CONGRESS CATALOGING-IN-PUBLICATION DATA
Names: Weinstein, Mobee, author.
Title: The complete book of ferns : indoors — outdoors — growing — crafting — history & lore / Mobee Weinstein.
Description: Beverly, Massachusetts : Cool Springs Press, 2019. | Includes index.
Identifiers: LCCN 2019032527 (print) | LCCN 2019032528 (ebook) | ISBN 9780760363942 (hardback) | ISBN 9780760363959 (ebook)
Subjects: LCSH: Ferns.
Classification: LCC QK522 .W45 2019 (print) | LCC QK522 (ebook) | DDC 587/.3—dc23
LC record available at https://lccn.loc.gov/2019032527
LC ebook record available at https://lccn.loc.gov/2019032528

Design and page layout: Laura Shaw Design, Inc.
Cover Image: Christina Bohn Photography
Printed in China

Dedicated to my mother,

Sue Clark

Contents

Acknowledgments

I am a true New Yorker and a representative of the New York fern, *Thelypteris noveboracensis*. The fronds of the New York fern can be recognized as tapering at both ends. To make this easy to remember, we affectionately describe it as a typical New Yorker, "burning the candle at both ends."

It is a privilege and a joy to write this book on ferns. My passion for plants goes back as far as I can remember. When I was growing up in the Bronx, my mother regularly took my sisters and me to visit the New York Botanical Garden (NYBG). She even told me it was my backyard. It's no surprise that I later studied at the NYBG School of Horticulture and continue to work there. Early on, I was assigned to take care of the fern house in the conservatory. The fern gallery was very large and lush, and a favorite of most visitors. As with all my assignments, the plants fascinated me (as they do to this day). I loved growing them and I wanted to learn everything about them. The more I learned, the more fascinating they became. Not only did the NYBG have an extensive collection of living ferns, but it also had a fern botanist on staff. It was my great fortune to work and study with Curator of Ferns Dr. John T. Mickel.

I also had the great privilege to work with and learn from the late Joe Beitel, another pteridologist on staff. I am honored to know the current Curator of Ferns Dr. Robbin Moran, who is always generous with his knowledge and ready to answer any question. John (and later Robbin) also ran the meetings for the New York Chapter of the American Fern Society, which were held at the NYBG. I became a member, and even served as vice-president and president. I am grateful to have met so many botanists, horticulturists, gardeners, and fern enthusiasts through the New York Chapter of the American Fern Society and the British Pteridological Society. Unfortunately, they are too many to name here. I thank them all for their dedication to studying and growing ferns and for generously sharing their knowledge. I would like to extend personal thanks to Judith Jones, Barbara Joe Hoshizaki, and Sue Olsen. I am lucky to have met them and learned from them. Their depth of knowledge, passion, and writings are inspiring. To Judith, thanks for many *frond* memories of frolicking through fern gardens, lingering up until the last minute.

Thanks to the New York Botanical Garden and Todd Forrest for allowing me to pursue this project.

I would also like to thank Marc Hachadourian for being my fellow plant geek at work, Corey Link for the tree cookies, and Gene Sekulow for sharing his and Yuji Yoshimura's bonsai soil recipes.

My sincere appreciation to Maria Colletti for introducing me to Mark Johanson and Cool Springs Press. Many thanks to Mark Johanson for starting this journey with me, and much gratitude to Jessica Walliser for seeing it through and finishing it with me. Thanks also to Heather Godin and the entire team at Cool Springs Press. You are an impressive bunch. Special thanks to photographer Christina Bohn for beautifully capturing all the DIY projects as well as some other images. Although we both worked very hard, it was so much fun!

I am most grateful to Matt Roberts and Ray Roberts of Central Florida Ferns for their generosity. This book would not have been possible without their incredible array of superbly grown ferns. Except for a few, all the ferns featured in Chapter 5 are theirs. Thanks also to Susan at cyanotypestore.com/store and Sally Muller at buylivingwalls.com for their help and generosity.

Finally, with all my heart, I thank my incredible family for a lifetime of love and support. Thanks to my sister Laura for her help with everything, from reading and editing to keeping me sane, to my sister Sharon for being the cheerleader, and to my aunt Sheila for the use of her dining room table, floss, and foil. To all my loved ones, who haven't seen much of me during this process, thank you for your patience and understanding. I love you all!

"The bright colours of flowers are admired by the least intellectual but the beauty of form and texture requires a higher degree of mental perception, and a more cultivated intellect for its proper appreciation. Hence we regard the growing taste for the cultivation of ferns as proof of mental advancement."

—From a fern catalogue issued in 1858 by fern nurseryman Abraham Stansfield, encomium by John Palmer

Welcome to the wonderful world of ferns!

CHAPTER 1

History, Lore, and Uses

ALTHOUGH FERNS MAY SEEM SIMPLE AND unassuming, especially when compared to the blooms of showy flowering plants such as colorful hibiscus or fragrant roses, they are among the world's greatest evolutionary success stories. Ferns have been part of the Earth's many ecosystems for hundreds of millions of years. You may find it hard to believe, but that small, feathery fern tucked in the corner of your garden, and the potted fern sitting on your bookshelf, are anything but simple. Ferns are tough, complex characters. Through changing climates, moving continents, and mass extinctions, ferns have carried on steadily and mostly unfazed. It's no wonder they've been used and appreciated by humans throughout our shared history. And it's no wonder that we humans continue to cultivate and adore ferns. Today, ferns are in the midst of a modern renaissance. Thanks to the continued rise in the popularity of houseplants, coupled with the adaptability, diversity, and aesthetics of ferns, this amazing group of plants graces our homes and

gardens with greenery and texture, and will no doubt continue to do so for generations to come.

Let's start by taking an in-depth look at the evolutionary history of ferns and learning why they are such successful plants. Then, we'll examine the inner workings of their life cycles, their myriad of forms, growth habits, and favored growing climates, and information on how to propagate these unique plants. In Chapters 3 and 4, you'll discover profiles of more than 70 popular indoor and out-door fern species, and care information to cultivate these plants in your home or landscape. The final chapter is dedicated to creative planting projects for growing ferns in some pretty surprising and inspired ways, along with a handful of techniques for turning ferns into works of art you can proudly display in your home.

Understanding how ferns came to be and the role these plants played in the evolution of the Earth we know today is the first step on our fern journey.

The Evolution of Ferns

You might be tempted to think ferns are primitive simply because they've been around for so long, and they may at first seem unremarkable. But ferns are prime examples of finding a winning formula and sticking with it. The interrupted fern, *Claytosmunda claytoniana* (syn. *Osmunda claytoniana*), for example, which is currently part of the native flora in eastern Asia and eastern North America and is at home in gardens as well as wild spaces, is a textbook illustration. Fossils of this exact fern have been found to be at least 180 million years old. By every measure, right down to the level of the fossilized cells, the modern interrupted fern appears to be totally unchanged after all those eons. Not only would this fern have been just as familiar to *Tyrannosaurus rex* as it is to us, but it had been growing happily for more than 100 million years before *T. rex* even appeared on the scene.

The history of evolving plant life has been marked by several important changes. Ferns are in a group of plants known as the seedless vascular plants, meaning they have one of the biggest innovations of plant life (vascular tissue), but lack another (flowers and seeds). To understand how ferns evolved, we first have to look at how the simplest of plants came to be and how those plants went on to change and evolve.

SIMPLE ORGANISMS

Some of the simpler organisms are the single-celled green algae, which generally make their living floating in water and photosynthesizing. Eventually, those single cells began to form larger, multi-celled organisms often called seaweed. Algae were likely the first land inhabitants living in a wet film and they are believed to have given rise to the increasingly more complex earliest land plants, liverworts and mosses. These are the earlier, nonvascular plants, which means they lack a vascular system to move water from one part of the plant to another. For algae living in the water, this is

obviously not a problem, but for nonvascular plants on the land, such as mosses, the lack of a vascular system significantly restricts the size of the plant. Mosses can soak up water like a sponge, but their lack of a system to pump water up from the ground means they can't support tall stems or wide leaves. As a result, mosses remain low, ground-hugging cushions.

VASCULAR PLANTS

Plant life started to rise off the ground when the first vascular plants arrived on the scene some 425 million years ago. Vascular tissue, which consists of tiny tubes running up plant stems, sometimes further strengthened with the organic compound lignin, freed plants from clinging to the ground. Being tall is no great

◄ (opposite page) *Claytosmunda claytoniana* (syn. *Osmunda claytoniana*), the interrupted fern, has remained unchanged for 180 million years.

◄ Moss grows low to the ground because it lacks a vascular system to transport water, restricting the size of the plant.

▼ Tall vascular plants and the first ferns began to inhabit the Earth hundreds of millions of years ago.

virtue on its own, but when a plant is fighting with other plants for valuable sunlight, height allows it to shade out the competition. Nonvascular plants, which had been happily forming green carpets basking in the sun, suddenly had to adjust to living in the deep shade of their taller competitors, or extreme conditions in which their tall relatives couldn't survive. Mosses, liverworts, and their kin got pushed to the sidelines over the next several million years as vascular plants quickly dominated the surface of the Earth, towering 100 to 150 feet (30.5 to 46 m) in the air. It is at this time that the first ferns made their appearance.

This explosion of lignin-reinforced vascular tubes enabled plants to reach soaring heights, creating the first forests. These massive forests in turn created an important facet of our modern world: coal. The era of seedless forests was also a time of very active plate tectonics. Continents were crashing into each other, pushing up mountain ranges and burying some of those new forests deep underground, transforming their trunks and foliage into the coal that fueled the Industrial Revolution.

SEED PLANTS

The next big evolutionary change in plants left ferns behind. The first seed plants arrived on the scene some 350 million years ago. Ferns and other seedless plants such as mosses reproduce via spores (more about this reproductive strategy in Chapter 2). Each tiny spore is fragile, requiring constant moisture to germinate and produce another generation of ferns. Seeds, on the other hand, give a baby plant a start-up package. Inside each seed is an embryo and, almost

▶ Most ferns survive under the canopy of larger trees thanks to a special gene for a light-sensing protein called neochrome, which allows the plant to respond to the presence of red light.

always, a supply of food; when a seed germinates, it has time to develop an initial root to harvest water before it begins to photosynthesize. This technique of giving baby plants a head start in life was wildly successful and allowed forests of conifers to dominate the landscape.

Ferns don't produce seeds or flowers, and like the mosses before them, they've lost their dominant hold on the planet. But ferns are still everywhere, growing in the shade of forest trees, thriving in cracks of rocks in deserts, floating in water, perched on the branches of towering trees, or vining up 50-foot (15 m) tree trunks. Although ferns today are not as numerous as seed plants, they are certainly far from extinct.

THE SUCCESS OF FERNS

Why have ferns managed to remain so successful? That's a big question, and scientists are still unraveling the various threads of the story, but one important piece of the puzzle seems to be that around the same time flowering plants showed up on the scene, ferns acquired a new trait of their own. It's not as radical a change as making seeds, but this change is a key attribute that helped ferns thrive.

Around 180 million years ago, when some of our modern species of ferns first came into being, and shortly (evolutionarily speaking) before flowering plants began spreading their canopies over the world, some ferns acquired a special gene for a light-sensing protein called neochrome. Neochrome allows ferns to detect and respond to the presence of red light. Other plants have light-sensing proteins that help them orient their foliage to capture the most light for photosynthesis, but other plants can only detect blue light. This works great for plants growing in full sun, as blue light is efficiently used by chlorophyll and carries a lot of energy. But under the shade of tall trees, most of the blue light has been filtered out by the leaves above, leaving behind higher amounts of red light—red light that, though lower in energy than blue, can still be used for photosynthesis. Ferns can

▶ Bracken fern has had a long history with humanity, having been utilized for many purposes, from food to animal bedding.

detect it, thanks to their neochrome. It may be this unique adaptation that has allowed ferns to continue to thrive in the shade of their seed-producing relatives.

Ferns came by their redlight–sensing capability in a very unusual way. Rather than developing slowly over time by means of chance mutations in the usual way of evolution, the gene for neochrome was snatched in its entirety from a little mosslike plant called a hornwort. This process is called horizontal gene transfer. Every once in a while, genes move from one organism to another not by the controlled process of sex, but spontaneously through cell walls when two organisms are in close contact. Recently, human scientists have started inducing these kinds of gene movements between organisms via genetic engineering, but even without human intervention, genes occasionally move around on their own. Some 180 million years ago, ferns got very lucky, and a bit of DNA made the leap from a hornwort to an ancestor of many modern ferns. This new gene gave ferns the ability to "see" red light, giving them a unique advantage when growing in the shade of other plants. So when you choose the best fern for a deeply shaded corner of your garden, thank the hornwort for sharing this special gene.

Part of why this gene made the leap from hornworts to ferns has to do with the structure of the gene itself, as it has portions that resemble transposons, the so-called "jumping genes" that are known to move readily around genomes. But another reason may be because ferns don't have seeds. Seeds germinate as robust little plants, with thick walls and little chance for foreign DNA to slip in. Scientists have identified horizontal gene transfer in these higher plants, but it is almost all due to parasites or disease-causing organisms, not other plants that happen to be in the

neighborhood. The same is true of humans, by the way: Virtually all our genes come from our evolutionary ancestors, but we've also picked up a few odd genes from human diseases along the way.

Germinating spores, on the other hand, are tiny, fragile things, often in very close quarters with other germinating spores, and apparently at that stage, they're more open to picking up DNA from their surroundings. So the neochrome gene made the leap from hornwort to fern spore, and since then, it has

spread through many distantly related groups of ferns, giving them the ability to "see" red light and thrive beneath the deep shade cast by other plants.

The History of Humans and Ferns

Though ferns had been around for hundreds of millions of years before humans, our own relatively short history with these plants is rich and fascinating. Bracken fern, of the genus *Pteridium*, has had a tumultuous history with humans, shifting from a hero through much of its history to a villain more recently.

The bracken ferns are some of the most successful ferns in the world, found nearly everywhere except deserts and the polar regions. Long underground stems allow it to spread rapidly, covering large areas with colonies of fronds. Bracken ferns' preferred habitat is moorland, where their main competition is low-growing grasses and shrubs. Unlike many ferns that thrive in the shade of other plants, bracken has very large fronds, sometimes reaching 6 feet (1.8 m)

in height, tall enough to shade out many of its low-growing competitors.

The UK has abundant moorland, beloved by bracken fern, and bracken was once a much loved plant with a myriad of uses. One of the most basic was animal bedding in barns. The tough fronds hold up well over a long period, and they produce some known insecticidal compounds, so it is possible their use as animal bedding may have kept insect pests at bay as well. Bracken has also been traditionally used as mulch, covering the soil in gardens to suppress weed growth.

Perhaps the most interesting way humans have used bracken ferns is as food. Raw bracken is highly toxic. When animals (including humans) chew on young fronds, the fronds release cyanide. The fronds also contain two hormones that cause insects to molt repeatedly until they die. As if all that wasn't enough, bracken also contains an enzyme that breaks down thiamine (also known as vitamin B), so a diet of bracken can cause a fatal vitamin B deficiency. Despite all that, bracken ferns are part of traditional diets around the world. People steam the young fronds, called fiddleheads, when they first emerge and a variety of dishes are based on the starch found in the underground rhizomes (thick, rootlike structures). This use of a highly toxic plant as food is possible because the toxic compounds are broken down by heat. Raw bracken will kill you. Cooked bracken ferns are nontoxic—humans have been consuming them for thousands of years—but cooked bracken is now a suspected carcinogen. As a result, the attitude toward bracken is decidedly less positive than it was in the past. In the UK, where bracken is particularly common, there is even a Bracken Advisory Commission, focusing on the health risks of bracken, and there is concern about it taking over the moorlands used for grazing livestock and replacing the grasses with its toxic fronds.

THE VICTORIAN FERN CRAZE

Our relationships with other ferns may not carry the same health risks as bracken presents, but they still have had their dramatic ups and downs. One of the most extreme moments in the history of humans and ferns is the wild fad for ferns that took over Victorian England, called pteridomania, or the Victorian fern craze. At its height in the second half of the 1800s, this fad for ferns took many different forms, and apparently reached across social classes and sexes, even in the strictly hierarchical and sexist Victorian society.

The name *pteridomania* (*Pterido* derived from the Greek word for fern) appears to have been coined by Charles Kingsley in his book on natural history

entitled *Glaucus or The Wonders of the Shore*. The formal name actually arrived at the end of the fad, at which point the passion for fronds had taken many different forms. Fern lovers grew these plants in their gardens or indoors as houseplants. Others tramped over the countryside hoping to spot a species of fern they hadn't seen before and press one of the fronds between sheets of paper to keep a record of their fern viewings. Some of the fern lovers of the time sought out unusual variants on the normal form of ferns. Today we call these sports or mutations, but the Victorians colorfully called them "monstrosities." Despite the name, these odd forms with variously shaped fronds were prized and collected, with hundreds of different forms recorded during the era. Most of these oddities didn't survive much past the end of the fern craze, but you can still find a few Victorian monstrosities for sale, including the popular Victorian tatting fern (*Athyrium filix-femina* 'Frizelliae'), an odd but attractive variant of the common lady fern.

Besides the mania for actual living ferns, images of ferns became ubiquitous on everything from clothing to ironwork to ceramics. For decades, ferns reigned supreme in the consciousness of the residents of the United Kingdom.

The Wardian Case

We'll never know exactly what causes a fad like pteridomania to spring to life—wouldn't marketers love it if we did? But looking back, we can see a couple of innovations that seem to have fueled the rise of the fern craze. One was the Wardian case. A Wardian case looks like a miniature glass greenhouse and is essentially the earliest version of a terrarium. A doctor named Nathaniel Ward (hence the name) created the first of these terrariums by accident. He lived in London, where at the time, the air was so polluted by the coal fueling the Industrial Revolution that it poisoned and killed all the ferns in his garden. (Ironically, his ferns were being killed by coal derived from their prehistoric relatives, the first vascular plants.)

▶ Wardian cases, such as the one illustrated here, allowed plants to be transported long distances and protected sensitive plants from pollution.

Dr. Ward, as was not uncommon for educated men of his time, was something of an amateur scientist and was observing the cocoons of moths placed in sealed glass bottles. His planned observations of moths didn't turn up any exciting discoveries, but they set the stage for the happy accident for which he is still remembered. While observing his cocoons, he noticed a fern and a few other plants growing in a bit of soil in one of the sealed bottles, so he decided to keep it and see how long the plants could survive sealed up in glass. Not only did the completely sealed bottle keep the fern from drying out, it also protected it from the air pollution, and unlike the short-lived ferns in his garden, the fern in the bottle thrived for some four years, until the bottle's seal failed and allowed in toxic air pollution.

Inspired, Dr. Ward had a tightly sealed glass box built, and grew thriving ferns inside it. He published his findings in 1842 in a book titled *On the Growth of Plants in Closely Glazed Cases*.

The Wardian case went on to become a significant player on the world stage, primarily for its use in the successful transport of living plants over long sea

▶ Cliff-dwelling fern species were collected during the Victorian fern craze, leading to some species being over-collected and threatened.

 Though the wild ferns suffered the most during the Victorian fern craze, fern collecting was not without its risks to humans as well. There are two well-documented cases of people falling from cliffs while trying to collect ferns, one of whom survived and got the fern he was after, and one, named William Williams, who died. His body was found at the base of a cliff where the fern *Woodsia alpina* was known to grow. Interestingly, though there are plenty of stories of fragile, excitable young Victorian ladies fainting and tumbling from cliffs while in the grip of pterid-omania, these stories appear to be fictitious, reflecting more the sexist attitudes of the time than the actual casualties of an interest in ferns by young females. The only documented death is of William Williams.

voyages. Live plants rarely survived the long voyages to and from Asia and Australia, thanks to the great difficulty in providing them with enough light and fresh water and protecting them from the constant salt spray from the ocean. The Wardian case neatly solved those problems and allowed live plants to move around the world. This caused an explosion of diversity in gardens, but more significantly, made it possible for the British to smuggle tea plants out of China to establish tea plantations in British India, and move rubber trees from Brazil to establish rubber plantations in Ceylon, modern-day Sri Lanka. The invention of the Wardian case broke what had been

powerful monopolies on these important agricultural commodities.

While the Wardian case was reshaping global trade and agriculture, closer to home, they became stylish and popular features of Victorian drawing rooms, filled with ferns thriving in the clean, consistently moist air found inside.

New Species Discovery

Along with the Wardian case, two other factors helped create and sustain the fern craze. One was that ferns had been understudied up to this point in favor of flowering plants, meaning that new fern species and forms were still awaiting discovery around England. Lovers of natural history and botany didn't need to sail around the world to find new plants—they could find them right in the British Isles. This was further encouraged by the development of better roads and railways, which made it easier for amateur botanists and fern lovers to travel the length and breadth of their country in search of the rarest and most exciting ferns, complete with the tantalizing possibility of maybe, just maybe, discovering a new species or a strange monstrosity. Add in the appeal of a socially acceptable pastime that allowed young women the freedom of trips out to the countryside with friends, and it is little wonder that ferns took over the Victorian psyche.

This love of ferns was not without its downsides. Fern lovers were so aggressive in collecting specimens of their favorite ferns from the countryside that several species were nearly collected right out of existence. Species that once had a large population in the UK were reduced to almost nothing by the fern craze. Some remain endangered to this day. The fern laws proposed by some during the height of pteridomania to fight over-collection were never enacted in the UK. However, in 1869 Connecticut enacted the first plant conservation law in the United States after a surge in popularity of the Hartford fern (*Lygodium plamatum*) as a Christmas decoration. Ferns, and many other plants, are still vulnerable to being "loved to death" by modern gardeners who illegally collect them from the wild. Gardeners should still never dig ferns—or other plants—from the wild. Instead, purchase plants from reputable nurseries. You'll get healthier plants and wild populations will be unaffected.

Fern mania eventually subsided, but the pleasure of discovering the world of ferns remains. Like the Victorians, we can cultivate ferns indoors and out, collect odd variants (though hopefully we won't refer

One of the most unexpected fern uses comes not from a true fern, but a group of fernlike plants in the genus *Lycopodium* (you'll learn more about fernlike plants in Chapter 2). Called club-mosses, these plants produce spores instead of seeds, just like ferns. The spores of clubmosses have myriad uses. Clubmoss spores are tiny and have a high fat content, so a cloud of them thrown into the air is highly flammable, creating a very dramatic—but relatively safe—burst of flame. Historically, clubmoss spores were used to create flashes of light for photography, and they are still used in special effects on stage and film today. Nowadays the fine powder on latex gloves that makes it easier to pull them on is starch, but *Lycopodium* spores were once used for the same purpose.

to them as "monstrosities"!), travel to see unusual ferns growing in the wild, and perhaps even have the chance to identify a new species. Ferns remain an understudied group of plants, and new species are still being discovered. *Adiantum shastense*, a fern native to California, was only named in 2015, and *Gaga germonotta* and *Gaga monstraparva*, both named for pop superstar Lady Gaga, were named in 2012. As long as you are careful when looking for ferns growing on cliffs and leave wild ferns happily growing where they are, you too can enjoy all the pleasures of pteridomania.

FERN LORE

Ferns have long captured the human imagination and woven themselves into our myths and legends.

One myth in Eastern Europe is that of the "fern flower." Ferns, as you now know, are nonflowering, seedless plants, but according to the myth, the mystical fern flower appears once a year on the eve of the

summer solstice. Finding a fern flower is supposed to bring luck, riches, or magical powers. In many countries, young couples go into the woods to "search for the fern flower" but spend their time alone doing something totally different. In some traditions, the "fern flower" is thought of as the pregnancy that may result from these summer nights spent in the woods.

In England during the seventeenth century, it was believed that burning stands of bracken ferns would bring rain, and apparently this belief was strong enough that it was requested that no ferns be burned during a visit from King Charles I to ensure sunny weather during his travels. Before the eighteenth century, it was assumed that all plants reproduced from seed and ferns popping up all over without any seed were credited with the power of invisibility; therefore, anyone possessing a fern seed would be able to make themselves invisible. Shakespeare made note of this in *Henry IV*: "We have receipt of fern-seed, we walk invisible."

More generally, ferns have been associated with fairies and dark mysticism. Some say a stand of ferns completely covering the ground can be used to summon the fairy Puck, and stepping on a fern can cause you to get lost and drawn into the magical fairy world, perhaps never to return.

Ferns may not summon literal fairies or have actual magical powers, but if you spend some time with these fascinating plants, perhaps on midsummer night, their beauty and elegance may just transport you somewhere magical.

◄ Fiddleheads are a springtime delicacy in many parts of the world.

The Many Uses of Ferns

Ferns have been put to many uses by humans over our long history. We've been eating ferns for a long time, and many cultures around the world eat a wide variety of fern species, mostly harvesting the new fronds before they've fully unfolded, at the so-called "fiddlehead" stage. Bracken ferns are of course eaten this way, but quite a few other species are as well. In Taiwan and elsewhere in Asia, the fronds of the bird's nest fern (the genus *Asplenium*) are popular as a vegetable. These tropical ferns are popular as houseplants around the world, and their broad, leafy fronds are quite tasty as well.

Unfortunately, there is mounting evidence that many ferns, not just bracken fern, are possibly carcinogenic if eaten regularly, despite being tasty. If you want to indulge in fiddleheads, it is best to do so in moderation.

The stems of the *Equisetum* species, commonly called scouring rush or horsetail, contain silica and can be used to scour pots and pans. They can also be used to file wood and to make reeds for clarinets.

One type of aquatic fern, the genus *Azolla*, is an effective fertilizer. This tiny fern has a symbiotic relationship with a cyanobacterium that converts nitrogen in the atmosphere into a form that plants can use as fertilizer. Because *Azolla*, when partnered with its bacterial friend, can produce its own fertilizer, this little fern can become a pest, doubling its mass every few days and quickly covering large water surfaces. But the vigor of *Azolla* has been put to good use in Asian rice farming. Rice needs a lot of nitrogen to produce maximum yields, so farmers inoculate rice paddies with *Azolla*, encouraging it to spread rapidly and release its nitrogen bounty to the rice as it decomposes.

Azolla is attracting new attention from researchers, in part because of this humble little fern's history. Around 50 million years ago, the world was a very different place, and much warmer thanks to high levels of greenhouse gases in the atmosphere. The

Arctic Ocean was essentially a huge, warm lake—the perfect habitat for *Azolla* ferns. It was so perfect that *Azolla* formed thick mats, covering the surface of the water. *Azolla* ferns periodically died and sank below the surface, only to be replaced by new mats of this rapidly growing fern. This cycle continued for roughly a million years. When the *Azolla* sank, it took with it the carbon it had taken from the air to fuel photosynthesis. Over a million years, this amounted to an enormous quantity of carbon, enough so that the amount of carbon dioxide in the air was cut to about half what it had been before the age of *Azolla* began. The changes in Earth's climate are incredibly complex, but it is thought that this fern may have been part of why Earth shifted to a cooler climate cycle, leading to ice ages and eventually the climate we are familiar with today.

Although we might not be able to use massive amounts of *Azolla* to suck carbon directly out of the air to fight climate change today (and we don't have a million years to wait) researchers are finding new uses for this simple fern that might help us reduce our carbon footprint and live more lightly. In addition to its long history of use as a natural fertilizer, *Azolla* is now being used to filter and clean gray water. This little fern is also edible and highly nutritious, and its prodigious growth rate means that, with minimal inputs, it could become an easy food source for livestock.

Finally, ferns are, of course, used for their aesthetics. It's plain and simple—people like looking at ferns. Their intricate fronds, divided into smaller leaflets in a kind of fractal geometry, are beautiful examples of complex designs created from simple rules. The airy, lacy texture of many ferns evokes delicacy and fragility, but ferns are astonishingly tough, preceding and outlasting the reign of dinosaurs and the arrival and end of ice ages. Surely they'll outlast us as well.

We visit museums and travel to historic sites to view snippets of our own tiny place in Earth's history. When we plant ferns in the garden or in containers indoors, we get to live with some of the oldest organisms on the planet. Maybe if we all spent more time with ferns, we'd learn something of their secret to living with grace, beauty, and strength.

◄ *Azolla* is a water-dwelling, floating fern that once formed thick mats over parts of Earth's oceans. As layers of *Azolla* settled to the bottom, it captured carbon and may have helped change Earth's climate.

| CHAPTER 2 |

The Botany of Ferns

Often people "identify" a plant as a fern simply based on the appearance of delicate, lacy leaves. Although this may be characteristic of many ferns, it isn't the case for all, and its not a sufficient way to identify them. Some plants have a fernlike appearance but are not ferns. The asparagus fern, named partly for its fernlike looks, is a perfect example. It isn't an actual fern but rather an asparagus. And although it's related to the food that shares the first half of its common name, the asparagus fern is not edible either. Ferns have familiar plant parts (roots, stems, and leaves) and the ferns we all instantly recognize have lacy foliage, but they're quite diverse in their appearance. What all ferns have in common, however, is the fact that they do not make flowers, fruit, or seed. If you see a plant with a flower, fruit, or seed, you're not looking at a fern!

So how can you know whether a particular plant is a fern? And what, exactly, is a fern? Botanically speaking, a fern is "a vascular plant with megaphylls that reproduces by spore." Unless you've studied some botany, that definition is probably too technical to be helpful. To understand what makes a fern a fern, let's start by looking at the three terms mentioned in that botanical definition: *vascular*, *megaphyll*, and *spore*.

WHAT IS A VASCULAR PLANT?

A vascular plant is one that has a specialized internal system for transporting water, minerals, and food throughout the plant. Think of it as a kind of plumbing system. Most of the obvious and familiar plants found on Earth today are vascular plants. In addition to the ferns, all seed-producing plants share this trait. Seed-producing plants include all flowering plants, as well as conifers (cone-bearing plants such as pines, firs, spruces, and all their varied relatives). With rare exceptions, vascular plants are comprised of distinct parts: roots, stems, and leaves. In contrast, examples of nonvascular plants include the mosses.

WHAT IS A MEGAPHYLL?

Megaphyll is the botanical term for a type of leaf. Literally, it translates to "large leaf," but it's defined as a complex leaf with branching veins. Such leaves are

▲ Ferns are vascular plants that do not produce flowers, fruits, or seeds. Instead, they reproduce by spore.

SEED PLANTS
ANGIOSPERMS AND GYMNOSPERMS

Angiosperm and *gymnosperm* are terms used to describe the two basic groups of seed-producing plants.

➤ The **angiosperms** are commonly known as the flowering plants. Their flowers develop into fruits that contain seeds. Angiosperms are the most diverse and dominant group of plants on Earth today. Roses, water lilies, tulips, sunflowers, apples, and magnolias are but a few examples.

➤ The **gymnosperms** do not make flowers and therefore do not make fruit. Instead, their seeds rest on "naked" leaves, or scales, which are more typically clustered into cones. Gymnosperms, the oldest of the living seed plants, most likely came from ancient "seed ferns" and are probably the ancestors of modern flowering plants. Conifers such as pine, spruce, cypress, and redwood are examples of gymnosperms. Cycads, which are better known in tropical and subtropical climates, and the well-known ginkgo tree are also examples of gymnosperms. Another member of this group, *Ephedra*, is known for treating breathing problems (it's an ingredient in the medication Sudafed).

LYCOPHYTES
(FERN ALLIES)

Meet the lycophytes. Formerly referred to as *fern allies*, lycophytes are a group of plants that have a distinct evolutionary history from ferns, but they share many characteristics with them. Additionally, the cultural needs of these two groups of plants have much in common. For these reasons, fern enthusiasts also typically study and grow lycophytes. However, despite all their similarities, they are not closely related to ferns.

Experts from around the world joined forces several years ago and published a modern comprehensive classification of lycophytes and ferns. Increasing molecular data has revolutionized our understanding and has led to this new organization of what were known for so long as "fern allies" and ferns. Though not closely related, the lycophytes and ferns share features that no other plants share, being vascular and producing spores in a unique life cycle. *Equisetum* and *Psilotum*, which were previously considered fern allies (they lack macrophylls), are now considered to be ferns, while their former brethren remain together in the lycophytes.

not strangers to you. Even if you're not familiar with a particular fern leaf, when you look at the leaves of seed-producing plants, you're also looking at megaphylls. Just a few examples are the leaves of maple, oak, and pine trees, petunias, sunflowers, corn, and rice. While ferns have megaphylls, other similar-looking plants called lycophytes differ in that they have microphylls (see sidebar for more on fern allies). A microphyll ("small leaf") is simply a leaf with a single, unbranched vein. As their name implies, having a single, nonbranching vein greatly limits their size. So the broad, lacy leaves of a fern are megaphylls, while the narrow, almost scale-like leaves of clubmosses and spikemosses are microphylls.

◄ Ferns form spores in sporangia commonly found on the backs of their fronds.

WHAT IS A SPORE?

The ferns and lycophytes (see page 31) are the only vascular plants that reproduce by spore, not seed. Their spores are single cells. They're microscopic and cannot be seen with the naked eye (for a description and illustration of where spores fit in the fern life cycle, see "How Ferns Propagate" on page 38). Reproducing by spore is an ancestral trait, and the completion of the fern lifecycle is dependent on the presence of water. Unlike other vascular plants, ferns retained this feature from their ancestors, being among the earliest plants to make the transition from water onto land.

The lesser-developed mosses and their relatives also reproduce by spore, but remember, unlike ferns, they are not vascular. Green algae are ancient organisms that also reproduce by spore and are most likely the ancestors of mosses and ferns. Although ferns kept this trait from their past, they were the first plants to develop a vascular system. As discussed in Chapter 1, this very significant evolutionary development is still used by the plants of today's world.

Parts of a Fern Plant

Because they are vascular plants, the spore-producing ferns and lycophytes have the same basic vegetative parts as seed-producing plants (flowering plants, conifers, and their relatives). However, in ferns and lycophytes, the roots, stems, and leaves may take on different proportions, appearances, and names.

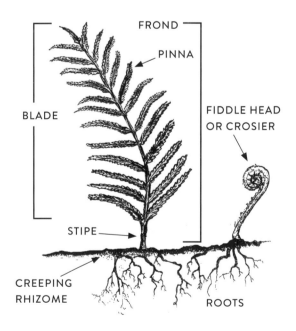

FROND

PINNA

BLADE

FIDDLE HEAD OR CROSIER

STIPE

CREEPING RHIZOME

ROOTS

▲ The illustration shows the many unique parts of a fern plant.

ROOTS

Roots, in any plant, can serve several basic functions. Moving through the soil or clinging to the branches of trees or surfaces of rocks, roots anchor ferns in place, keeping them from toppling over, washing away in a rainstorm, or blowing away in the wind. Another main function of roots is to absorb water and nutrients from the soil, delivering them through the fern's vascular system to all parts of the stem and fronds.

Not all roots serve all these functions. Epiphytic ferns, those that live perched on the branches of trees, often absorb most of their water and nutrients through their leaves, while the roots serve primarily just to hold them in place. Floating aquatic ferns, such as those in the genus *Azolla*, have given up staying in one place and float freely, using their roots just to help extract nutrients from the water they float on.

LEAVES

The leaves of ferns are called fronds. This word, usually reserved for the leaves of ferns, is sometimes applied to the similar-looking leaves of palms and cycads. Though fern fronds are structurally very similar to the leaves of other plants, there is a specialized vocabulary for describing their parts.

The main, broad part of the leaf is called the blade, and it is attached to the main stem of the fern by a stalk called a stipe. When most of us think of a fern frond, we imagine the classic look, with the blade divided into many tiny segments. Many ferns do indeed have that structure, but it is by no means universal. Fronds can range from simple, completely undivided leaves to multiple compound leaves, with the segments further divided into smaller segments, and everything in between.

In addition to their often finely divided shapes, the most iconic and distinctive aspect of fern fronds is the way almost all of them unfurl. Unlike the leaves of most other plants, new fern fronds emerge tightly coiled and then unroll to expose their intricate beauty. The tightly coiled fronds just beginning to unroll are called fiddleheads or crosiers. Named after the distinctive carved scroll at the top of a violin, the fiddlehead stage of frond development is when ferns are most often eaten as vegetables, and one of their most beautiful states. For gardeners in cold climates, the sight of fiddleheads pushing up from the ground ranks alongside daffodils and returning birds as a treasured sign of spring.

STEMS

The fronds and roots of ferns grow from the stems, called rhizomes. Fern rhizomes come in two types, creeping and erect. Creeping rhizomes run along or just below the soil surface and are how a fern spreads to cover a large or small area. Some ferns, such as bracken, have very long creeping rhizomes that allow them to quickly cover wide swaths of land. Others, such as the Japanese painted fern, have short creeping rhizomes, and so tend to stay in compact clumps. And there are still others in between that creep slowly and make patches. Some ferns have it multiple ways. Boston ferns, popular as houseplants, and ostrich ferns will make thick clumps with short rhizomes, but then send out stolons (modified stems) in order to expand their territory.

Individual fronds can grow from these creeping rhizomes, or the plants can grow what are called ascending or erect rhizomes. These very short stems produce an abundance of fronds in a clump, producing the classic vaselike grouping of leaves seen in ostrich ferns or the tropical bird's-nest fern.

The appearance of a fern and how it performs in the garden depend on the structure of the rhizomes. Plants with long creeping rhizomes, such as bracken, produce many individual fronds widely spaced over the ground. Japanese painted ferns have short creeping rhizomes, resulting in tight clumps of fronds that spread minimally. Ostrich ferns have erect rhizomes, resulting in the fronds radiating out into a graceful vase shape.

A few ferns take the erect rhizomes to a real extreme, producing the "tree" ferns. These dramatic rhizomes can grow taller than a person, producing a thick, hairy "trunk" with a ring of huge fronds growing at the top. These dramatic ferns are, unfortunately, not adapted to most climates, as they resent both cold winters and hot summers. But, where they will grow, they are incredible examples of the diversity and beauty of ferns.

Diversity in Ferns and Their Forms, Climates, and Lifestyles

When you imagine a fern growing in the wild, you probably imagine it growing on the ground, beneath the shade of tall trees. That is where we most often see ferns growing, in temperate and tropical climates and growing in shade is one of their unique adaptations. But shady woodlands aren't their only habitat. Ferns are incredibly varied and have found ways to adapt to conditions nearly everywhere on the planet.

There are many different habitats where ferns thrive, and many ways these plants grow.

- Terrestrial ferns live in the ground.

- Aquatic ferns live in or on the water.

- Epiphytic ferns live on the branches of trees.

- Epipetric and lithophytice ferns both grow on the surfaces of rocks.

Aquatic ferns grow in fresh, or sometimes brackish, water. Some of these ferns grow rooted to the bottom underwater, while others (such as the *Azolla* ferns) live a more freewheeling existence, floating on the water surface. At the other extreme are the xeric ferns, those adapted to live in arid climates with low humidity and rainfall. These dry-climate ferns tend to have thick, leathery fronds, often covered with silvery hairs or a waxy coating to help reflect some of the intense sunlight. They're beautiful, and though sometimes difficult to find for sale, make great additions to a water-wise landscape in areas with limited rainfall.

One fascinating fern relative that has adapted to extremes of climate is the so-called resurrection plant, *Selaginella lepidophylla*. Not a true fern, this little spikemoss is native to the Chihuahuan Desert in northern Mexico and the southwestern United States. Faced with long periods of drought, this little plant appears as if it dies. It turns brown, loses up to 95 percent of its water, and curls up into a ball. But it isn't dead—it simply goes dormant. It can remain in this dead-looking state for months, and when moisture returns, those dead-looking leaves unfurl, turn green, and get back to the business of photosynthesizing until the next time drought returns.

This ability to dry out without dying is shared by some true ferns as well. The resurrection fern (*Polypodium polypodioides*) is native to the southeastern United States, often in areas with extremely high rainfall. If you've visited Georgia or South Carolina in the summer and suffered in the high humidity, you would think nothing in the area dries out. However, this fern doesn't live in the soil. Instead it is an epiphyte found growing on the branches of trees, often high above the ground. Perching on the branch of an oak tree is a great way to get access to more light than is available on the forest floor, but it doesn't take much of a drought for this fern to dry out. And so, despite living in one of the rainiest parts of North America, these ferns are masters of surviving drought. Like the resurrection plant, the resurrection fern can lose nearly all its water, shrivel up, and turn brown, but still be just fine and rehydrate once rainy weather returns.

Growing on the branches of other plants, especially trees, is called epiphytism, and this is how many ferns grow. When people see one plant growing on another, they often think the plant is acting as a parasite, but epiphytes aren't parasites. They don't take any energy from the host plant they're growing on—they're just "borrowing" the trunk as a way to get off the ground and up into a little more light. But life clinging to a branch in the middle of the air is rough. Water can be hard to come by, and in temperate climates, epiphytes are exposed to the extremes of wind and cold, unmitigated by the shelter and warmth of the ground. For these reasons, most epiphytes of all kinds, including ferns, are found in tropical and subtropical regions, where winter cold isn't a problem, and regular rain and high humidity make life on a tree branch possible. But even so, many epiphytic ferns share traits with plants adapted to deserts. The

◀ Xeric ferns, such as this lace-lip fern (*Cheilanthes*), are adapted to live in dry climates and rocky areas.

▼ Resurrection ferns are epiphytes that appear to be dead during times of drought. However, when rain returns, they spring back to life.

bird's-nest fern is an epiphytic fern and is quite popular as a houseplant. It has thick, leathery, glossy leaves that help minimize moisture loss in the event of a short dry spell.

The great diversity of how ferns live in the wild is fascinating in its own right, and understanding a little of where a fern comes from can be a huge help in understanding the conditions it needs to live happily in your home or garden.

How Ferns Propagate

Propagation is how one fern plant can make more ferns. This happens in the wild as ferns naturally spread and reproduce via spores, and there are simple techniques we gardeners can use to speed up that process and make more ferns to fill our homes and gardens.

ASEXUAL AND SEXUAL PROPAGATION

There are two ways ferns propagate: sexually and asexually (also called vegetative propagation). Sexual reproduction is something I'm sure you are familiar with, though ferns do it a little—okay, a lot—differently than animals, namely through their spores. Getting the right conditions for fern spores to germinate and develop into a new fern can be a bit tricky for beginning gardeners, but it is the best way to propagate large numbers of new ferns. Each new plant grown from spores will be genetically a little different, combining traits from both parents, which can be very interesting and fun, particularly with highly variable species such as Japanese painted ferns.

Asexual or vegetative propagation is a lot simpler and can be as easy as physically dividing a plant in half. You'll usually be able to produce only a few new plants at a time this way, and unlike with sexual propagation, each new plant will be genetically identical (a clone) of the original plant. Here's more on both types of fern propagation.

SEXUAL REPRODUCTION AND THE FERN LIFE CYCLE

Sexual reproduction—in plants and animals—occurs when an organism produces cells with half as many chromosomes as the organism itself. Those cells are eggs and sperm. An egg carrying half the chromosomes from one parent fuses with the sperm carrying half the chromosomes from another parent. The fusion of the two sex cells produces a new cell with a full complement of chromosomes, half from each parent, thereby combining into a new generation with a new combination of genes.

Ferns, unlike animals, have a complex life cycle called alternating generations. The fern plants with big fronds that you're familiar with growing in the garden don't produce sex cells. They produce spores, and those spores have half of the chromosomes. But spores don't fuse together—they develop into little plants of their own. Spores grow into a distinct, free-living, and photosynthesizing tiny plant called the gametophyte (the sexual generation). In almost all ferns, this tiny fern will produce both the male and female sex cells (gametes, each still with half of the chromosomes). Once the plant is big enough, it will begin to make egg and sperm cells. The sperm swims through a thin film of water to an egg and if all goes well, they will combine and form a new fern. This baby is the new sporophyte generation and the cycle is complete. The tiny gametophyte plant only lives to produce one fertilized egg and then it will die.

This means that ferns live in two distinct stages. The familiar stage you see growing in your garden is called the *sporophyte*, which means "spore plant." Sporophytes grow over a long period, and when mature, they begin producing structures called sporangia. Most often the sporangia,which look like little brown or black raised bumps, are in clusters called sori and are found on the undersides of the fronds. They release tiny spores, which float like dust in the air, drifting everywhere and hopefully settling in a suitable moist spot.

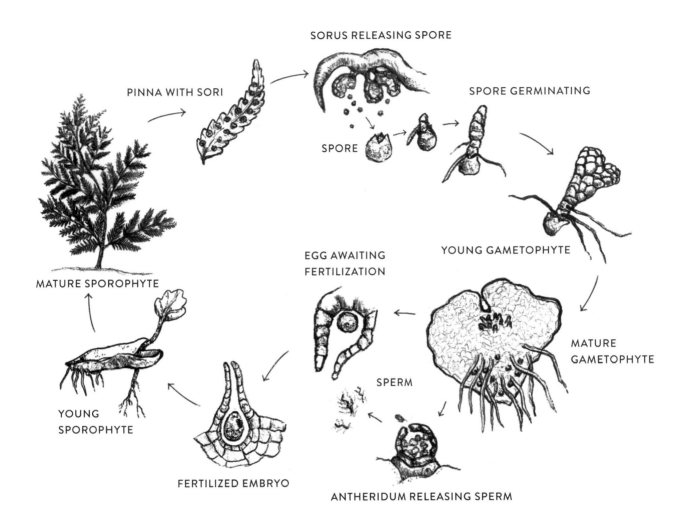

SORUS RELEASING SPORE

PINNA WITH SORI

SPORE GERMINATING

SPORE

YOUNG GAMETOPHYTE

MATURE SPOROPHYTE

EGG AWAITING
FERTILIZATION

MATURE
GAMETOPHYTE

YOUNG
SPOROPHYTE

SPERM

FERTILIZED EMBRYO

ANTHERIDUM RELEASING SPERM

▲ This illustration shows the complete fern life cycle, starting with the recognizable sporophyte you see in your garden, through the production and germination of microscopic spores, the development of the gametophyte that produces sperm and eggs, and finally the production of a new, young sporophyte.

Given the right conditions, spores will germinate and grow into new gametophytes. As discussed earlier, these tiny little plants produce gametes (eggs and sperm), which fuse and produce new ferns. If the spores from different individual ferns land in the same area, they can cross-fertilize and recombine the genes of the two parent ferns. This is worth remembering if you want to sow out your own ferns via spore. If, for example, you have a large collection of different varieties of Japanese painted ferns, you could sow all the spores together to encourage genetic recombination and produce diverse new fern babies. Or you could keep the varieties separate in hopes of producing babies that look like the plants you already have.

▲ A microscopic view of a tiny fern gametophyte with its new baby sporophyte.

Ferns of different species can hybridize when their spores grow together. The variety *Athyrium* 'Ghost' is just such a hybrid, produced when a Japanese painted fern native to Asia and the lady fern, native to North America, had their spores exchange gametes. The result is a fern that combines some of the traits of the two parents. Fern hybrids between different species, but usually in the same genus, are known to gardeners and even in the wild, so if you want to play around with sowing different spores together, you might get lucky and create an interesting new plant.

◀ Sporangia are usually clustered into a sorus (plural: sori), which is commonly found on the undersides of fern fronds. Sori look like little raised bumps.

HOW TO PROPAGATE FERNS THROUGH SPORES

In nature, mature ferns produce spores by the thousands, if not millions, every year. Often none or only one or two of those spores will get lucky and land in just the right spot to germinate and produce a new fern. Those odds work for ferns over the long term, but for the gardener looking to produce a batch of new ferns from spores, it is best to give the spores the special care required for a much higher success rate. The process of sowing your own spores isn't too complex, but it does require some careful attention to details.

MATERIALS NEEDED

- Fern frond with sporangia
- White sheets of paper and a heavy book
- Small glass container
- Larger glass bowl for water
- Chlorine bleach
- Clean paper towel

- Compressed peat pellet
- Kettle of boiling water, preferably distilled
- High quality potting soil or vermiculite
- Small piece of plastic wrap
- Rubber band
- Pin

STEP 1

Choice A: Collect spores.

The exact time to do this will be different with every fern. In general, what you'll be looking for are very dark brown or black raised bumps on the underside of the fern fronds or special dedicated "fertile fronds," which aren't green, but instead very dark brown or black. (Note that at maturity, some species are golden and others are green.) When the sori look ripe, cut the frond off the plant and lay it on a sheet of white paper. Cover the paper with another piece of paper and place a book on top to keep it from moving or being exposed to air movement. Over the next few days, you should see a brown (or occasionally gold or green) powder collecting on the paper under the frond. Those particles are the spores! If no spores are released, you might have collected the fronds too early or too late. You can always try collecting fronds at different stages of development until you find the best time for your favorite fern.

Choice B: Purchase spores.

If you don't want to collect your own spores, you can also purchase them from a few sources. Fern spores are never widely available, but if you can find them for sale, they can be a great, affordable way to increase your fern collection if you have a little patience. Joining a fern society is another way to access the spores of many interesting species.

Most spores can be stored dry for quite a long time, just like seeds. Seal them in an envelope and store in a cool dark place such as a refrigerator until you are ready to plant them. However, ferns that produce green spores need to be sown right away. The green spores are photosynthetic and will die in long storage. Some fern growers have successfully stored green spores and had them germinate, but as a rule, fresh is best, especially if the spores are green.

STEP 2 | Sterilize the glass container.

To sow your spores, start by sterilizing a small glass container by dipping it in a 10 percent solution of chlorine bleach and water (one part bleach to nine parts water), making sure it's thoroughly washed inside and out. Remove it carefully and set it upside down to dry on a clean paper towel.

STEP 3 | Prepare the peat pellet.

Next, peel the netting back from the center of the peat pellet and place the compressed peat pellet in the sterilized glass container, and pour in boiling water from a kettle. The hot water will cause the compacted pellet to expand and rehydrate and help sterilize the soil. Alternatively, you can put a layer of moist, but not sopping wet, potting soil or vermiculite in the bottom of the glass container (don't use soil from your garden; it will have too many weed seeds and possible pathogens) and then microwave the container of soil for a couple of minutes to sterilize. After either method, immediately cover the container tightly with a layer of plastic wrap and let cool completely.

STEP 4 | Sow the spores.

When your peat pellet has expanded and cooled, check for standing water. Peel back a corner of the plastic to pour out any excess water. Transfer the spores to a clean, sharply folded piece of paper. When ready, peel back the plastic and gently tap the paper, sprinkling the spores all over the top of the pellet.

STEP 5 | Cover the container.

Immediately re-cover with the plastic and secure with a rubber band. Place it where it will get light (even house lighting) but no direct sun. The sealed container will act like a tiny greenhouse and quickly overheat if direct sun shines on it. If you have grow lights for starting seedlings indoors, those will work great. Average house warmth is ideal.

STEP 6 | Keep the spores moist.

Your mini greenhouse should stay sufficiently moist. Seeing some condensation on the inside is a good sign. If it starts to dry out, boil water, cover it as it cools down, and then carefully peel back just a corner of the plastic and pour a tiny bit of the water inside and re-cover immediately. After the first month if you see growth, gently tap on the top of the plastic every couple of days to knock some of the drops of water onto the developing gametophytes to aid in fertilization.

STEP 7 | Transplant the young ferns.

After another month or more, if all has gone well, you should start to see tiny fronds beginning to stick up. These are your baby sporophytes. Once the baby ferns are big enough to handle, transplant them out into individual containers and cover them with plastic wrap. After a few weeks, poke a few tiny pin holes in the plastic. Every 3 to 5 days, poke a few more holes in the plastic. After several weeks your baby ferns should be ready for you to remove the plastic. Keep moving them into bigger containers as they grow, and after 6 months to a year they should be big enough to be planted out in your garden or share with your friends. Remember that every new fern grown from spores will be genetically different, so as they grow, take time to look them over and pick your favorites, which may be the individuals that grow the most vigorously or have the best color in their fronds.

HOW TO PROPAGATE FERNS THROUGH ASEXUAL PROPAGATION

If you've ever come across a big patch of ferns in the woods, you've probably seen an example of asexual propagation. Nearly all ferns, after they grow from spores, will begin to spread by means of their creeping rhizomes, one plant growing over time into a whole colony. As a gardener, you can take advantage of this to multiply your ferns quickly and with less fuss than growing from spores. There are several different ways you can propagate ferns asexually.

Propagation by Division

Physically dividing ferns is the simplest way to propagate them. Simply take a mature clump of ferns out of its container or dig it up out of the ground and divide it into pieces. Every separate clump of fronds—growing on an erect rhizome—can be separated out into an individual plant.

For some creeping species, you can simply pull the clump apart with your hands. Others may have strong rhizomes that need to be cut apart with a sharp knife, pruning shears, or shovel. Once you've cut the rhizome, pull the plants apart to untangle their roots.

Once they're separated, replant each divided section either in containers or in the ground. Be sure to keep new divisions well watered for the first few months after dividing them while they reestablish themselves.

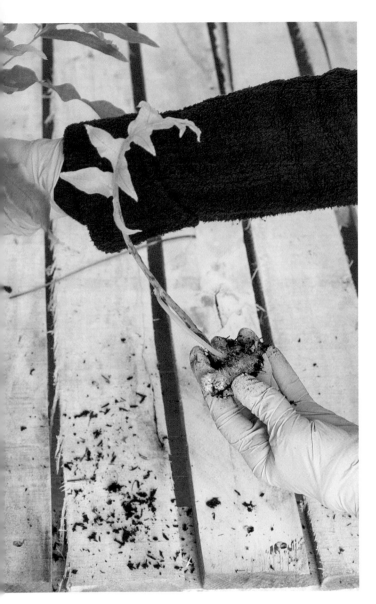

Propagation by Rhizome Cuttings

Fern varieties such as the rabbit's foot fern, a popular houseplant, that grow long rhizomes on the soil surface or beneath can be cut off to propagate the plant. Cut sections of rhizome that have at least one frond attached and a growing tip and place them on the surface of a pot of moist soil or long fiber sphagnum moss. Keep them shaded and provide high humidity for the best results.

Alternatively, cover the newly planted rhizome with a glass cloche or a plastic beverage bottle with the bottom cut off to keep the humidity high and the soil moist.

Propagation by Proliferations (Bulbils)

A few types of ferns can be propagated in a very unusual way, from small growths on the fronds themselves. Called proliferations or bulbils, these look like small bumps or knots on the frond, often with a smaller frond growing up from them. To propagate fern species that produce them, simply cut a frond with bulbils off the plant, lay it flat on the surface of a container of moist soil, and keep in high humidity and shade until they grow roots. Alternatively, place a glass or plastic cloche over the container to retain moisture and humidity.

Though generally you can grow new plants from fronds only if you see bulbils forming, a few ferns that are capable but haven't produced bulbils can be induced to do so. The beautiful lacy fronds of *Polystichum setiferum*, if placed on moist soil and kept in bright, shaded, humid conditions, will often grow new plantlets along the length of the frond.

Botanical Names and What They Mean

Ferns, like most organisms, usually go by at least two different names: a common name and a scientific botanical name (sometimes called a Latin name, though scientific names are often a mixture of Latin, Greek, and made-up words).

The furry creature curled up on your sofa can be called a house cat (the common name) or *Felis catus* (the scientific name). The same goes for your ferns. Let's use an example I've used before, the Japanese painted fern. The pretty little silvery fern in your garden can be called a Japanese painted fern or *Athyrium niponicum* (Pictum). The advantage of common names is that they are usually easy to remember, say, and spell, but the disadvantage is that they are essentially informal nicknames, and the same plant may have different common names in different places. Conversely, different plants may have the same common name, making things very confusing. Obviously, this common name is only used in English-speaking countries. The common name of this plant would be something completely different in a non-English-speaking region. Scientific names, however, are more precise, and *Athyrium niponicum* (Pictum) always means the same plant, no matter where in the world you go and what language is spoken there.

Scientific names are made up of two parts: the genus and the specific epithet (often incorrectly called the species). The first part, *Athyrium*, is the genus, and refers to a group of related species. Tack on the specific epithet, and the name refers to a specific species. So *Athyrium niponicum* (Pictum) is the Japanese painted fern, while *Athyrium filix-femina* is the closely related lady fern, and *Athyrium* on its own refers to the whole genus, which includes some 180 different species, most of which are not commonly grown in gardens.

▼ This cultivar of *Athyrium niponicum* has traits that other varieties do not, so it bears an additional name to distinguish it from other varieties.

There can be other names tacked onto the end of the basic scientific name. For example, *Athyrium filix-femina* var. *angustum*: "Var." is short for variety, and it refers to a distinct variant on the basic species. In this case, variety *angustum* has red stalks and is a popular garden fern. You might also see "subsp.," short for subspecies. This again refers to a distinct group within the species.

Finally, at the end of the scientific name, you might see another name in single quotes, for example *Osmunda regalis* var. *regalis* 'Purpurascens'. The last name, always in single quotes, is a cultivar name. Cultivar is short for cultivated variety and means a specific individual that a gardener or nursery grower selected for being distinct and interesting.

In summary, *Osmunda* is a genus, made up of about four species; *regalis* is a widespread species native to North America, tropical America, and Europe; var. *regalis* is the variant native to Europe; and 'Purpurascens' is a specific plant, in this case with wine purple coloring on the stalks.

Sometimes you will see a scientific name that is just a genus and a cultivar name, for example, *Athyrium* 'Ghost'. This beautiful fern is a hybrid, and since one parent is *Athyrium niponicum* 'Pictum' and the other parent is *Athyrium filix-femina*, it doesn't belong to either species, so it is just referred to by the genus, and then a cultivar name attached to that particular individual.

In theory, scientific names are precise, reliable, and universal. In practice, they do change, and in recent years they've been changing a lot. Scientific names are supposed to be based on actual evolutionary and genetic relationships, so scientists would like all plants called *Athyrium* to be more genetically like each other than they are to ferns placed in a different

genus. Historically, they've decided how to classify ferns and other organisms by looking at them closely and deciding which shared characteristics indicate the closest evolutionary and genetic relationship. For example, whales have fins and live in the ocean, but since they breathe air and produce milk, scientists have long considered them more closely related to dogs and bears than to fish.

To unravel relationships in the world of ferns, scientists look closely at the structure of the fronds, rhizomes, spores, sporangia, and gametophytes. Those are all open to interpretation, so different scientists sometimes disagree on the best way to classify things. To add to the chaos, in recent years DNA sequencing has been added to the toolkit, and that has resulted in a lot of scientists arguing for new classifications and scientific names. So, though most gardeners still use the name *Athyrium*, some scientists now call lady ferns and Japanese painted ferns *Anisocampium*. These name changes can be frustrating for gardeners, but hopefully once the DNA-based renamings work their way through the system, the new names will stay more stable for a while. And keep in mind that there is no "official" scientific name for any plant. Like all of science, plant taxonomy is a debate about best evidence. Each researcher makes the case for the names and organization of plants that they think make sense based on their research, and if other scientists agree, they start using those names. If not, they don't. Over time, this produces a consensus regarding which scientific names to use.

Despite the occasional name changes, scientific names are still the most reliable way to communicate about ferns with other fern lovers, avoiding the confusion that can often result from relying on common names.

Now that you understand the fascinating evolutionary history of ferns, their growth habits and forms, and the basics of their life cycle and propagation, let's turn our attention to some of the best fern species to grow in our homes and gardens.

◄ Scientists look closely at the structures of a fern, including their rhizomes, fronds, spores, sporangia, and more to help classify and name them.

CHAPTER 3

Greening Your Environment

FERNS INDOORS

FERNS ARE SOME OF THE MOST BEAUTIFUL houseplants, providing delicate, lacy qualities, classic forms, and rich textural variety. They are also masters of the color green, showing off its whole range, and displaying variations from gray to blue to chartreuse, and even red and silver. You'll find ferns for the smallest of spaces all the way up to big, bold specimens. There are ferns for every interior style, be it formal décor, casual, or a sleek, modern look. These are not your grandmother's houseplants! Ferns will also reward you as they connect you to nature, bringing the green world indoors. Take a moment and contemplate them. Just exactly what shade of green do you see? What is the texture of the frond like? You'll enjoy the excitement of seeing new growth unfurl before your eyes, and you can breathe healthier indoor air because of the presence of these beautiful plants.

Growers are expanding their listings and offering a wider assortment of ferns that grow well indoors. When buying your plants, always buy from reputable sources. Plants grown in good nurseries will be healthy, should be ethically grown and sourced, are not collected in the wild, and will generally be free from pests. In any case, give them a good examination before you buy them, and if you can, quarantine them briefly when you get them home to make sure that they have no pests that might spread to other plants. Keep in mind that any indoor setting, including a home, office, or school, is an artificial environment. It is best to assess your indoor conditions and then select

No space? No problem! Pint-size ferns are the perfect fit for tiny living quarters. Left to right: A baby staghorn fern mounted on a tiny tree round, a small, young potted Tsus-sima holly fern, a sporeling of button fern in a thimble, and a lemon button fern in a moss-lined wire cap cover from a prosecco bottle.

an appropriate plant. This is a helpful first step to success. It is usually difficult to change your environment to suit the plant, though, as you will see, there are some adjustments you can make.

GROWING CULTURE

When choosing which ferns to grow as houseplants, it can be helpful to have a look at their natural habitat for clues to their specific growing needs. There are five cultural factors that you need to consider when growing ferns, or any plant for that matter:

- ➤ Light

- ➤ Temperature

- ➤ Growing medium or substrate (soil, soilless mix, potting mix)

- ➤ Watering

- ➤ Humidity

Individually, these factors are like pieces of a puzzle. When you put them all together, you get the complete picture. Because they are all interrelated, changes in one factor may very well affect one or more of the other factors. Another way to explain this is to think of a chain made up of individual links; each of these five factors is a link. Your chain will only be as strong as the weakest link. To keep your ferns thriving, make sure that the environment and your culture match the needs of your plant.

LIGHT

Light is critical for all green plants and is one of the hardest things to get right in any indoor setting.

Ferns generally want medium light, or bright, indirect light, but not burning sun. Most ferns do very well in an eastern light exposure. For western exposures, you need to be more careful—afternoon sun can be too strong and hot. For northern and southern exposures, it matters whether you are in the Northern or the Southern Hemisphere.

In the Northern Hemisphere (north of the equator), a northern exposure in the winter is generally too dark, and even in the summer it often doesn't provide enough light in an average indoor setting. A southern exposure is typically too sunny and hot in the summer, but it can be good for the winter. In the Southern Hemisphere (south of the equator), it is the opposite. A north-facing window will often be fine for your ferns in winter, but in summer it can be too strong. A south-facing window will generally be too dark, especially during the winter. Therefore, you need to consider the north- and south-facing settings accordingly. The east- and west-facing settings are not reversed based on which hemisphere you are located in. Another important consideration that can affect seasonal light is latitude, that is, how near or far you are from the equator. The sun's light is consistent all year round at the equator. The farther you get from the equator, either north or south, the greater the seasonal change in light. As you move away from the equator, the longer your days are in summer, the stronger the sun. Conversely, during winter months, the shorter the day length, the weaker the sun's intensity. If your setting is much darker during this season, other brighter exposures are often helpful, but I find east to be good year-round as long as these exposures are unobstructed.

As a general guide:

- ➤ In the Northern Hemisphere, northern exposures are lowest light, east and west are medium, and southern exposures are high.

- ➤ In the Southern Hemisphere, southern exposures are the lowest light, east and west are medium, and northern exposures are high.

Observe the light as it comes into your home to get a better understanding of the best place for your plants. For east and west exposures, the light generally comes in at an angle when the sun rises in the morning in the east or as it sets in the west. This means you can get light farther into the room and sometimes place plants farther back from your windows. East and west typically afford medium light, sufficient for ferns, but close to the window can border on too intense. Ferns on a windowsill in a western setting could get too hot.

It might also be possible to grow ferns in some of the stronger light settings if other conditions are affecting the light. Obstructions outside such as trees or tall buildings that block light, having sheer curtains that soften the light, or placing your ferns far enough back from the window might reduce the light to a desirable level. Contrary to an unfounded but common belief, ferns do not grow in the dark. Your indoor setting can also affect light levels. Lighter walls reflect more sunlight and can help, and you can also use mirrors to help reflect light. Dark walls will make your room darker and reflect less light to your plants. Keeping your windows clean can make quite a difference, too.

Observe your plants once they are in place, watching for symptoms that indicate too little or too much light (see "Troubleshooting Guide" on page 78). If the light comes from one direction, you may notice your fern leaning toward the light. To correct this problem and keep your plant in even form, rotate your pot one-quarter turn every week. Pay attention to your plants—they'll let you know when they're happy and when they're not.

TEMPERATURE

Most of the ferns grown indoors are tropical in nature and generally grow well with daytime temperatures of 70 to 80°F (21 to 27°C). On a hot summer day, many handle temperatures as high as 90°F (32°C), but that's not desirable. They also prefer at least a

Pay careful attention to light levels when choosing a home for your fern.

5 to 10°F (2.8 to 5.6°C) difference between the daytime and nighttime temperatures. This temperature gradient gives your plants a nightly rest. Ferns are typically happy with nighttime temperatures of 60 to 65°F (16 to 18°C).

In winter, especially if light levels are lower, temperatures at the lower end of the range are better for your ferns. Although ferns growing on a windowsill might receive proper light, take notice of the temperature. Being next to the glass, they may get too hot during the day and/or too cold during the night. Keep in mind that, like most plants, ferns generally resent great fluctuations in temperature. Some indoor ferns are native to regions where they experience cooler temperatures, and these ferns might easily tolerate, or even prefer, temperatures as low as 50°F (10°C), possibly even 40°F (4°C), during winter nights. It is better not to subject a fern to such low temperatures unless you know it's a species that can handle it, or you are intentionally experimenting and are willing to lose your specimen! Ferns not suited to such low temperatures may well survive, but they'll let you know how unhappy they are. Their growth rate slows, damage may be evident, and they may be very slow to recover.

GROWING MEDIUM

The correct potting mix, or growing medium, is very important to the health of your fern plants. The growing medium is the substance in which the roots are growing. Roots take up water and nutrients for the fern, and roots need oxygen to survive. As ferns tend to have shallow, thin root systems, a well-aerated, well-drained potting mix is necessary. At the same time, the mix must hold sufficient moisture and nutrients. This balance is not that difficult to achieve, and it is vital. Most ferns, like most other plants, thrive in a slightly acidic medium with a pH between 6 and 7. Most ready-made potting mixes are adjusted to this proper pH range.

If your fern is thriving, you most likely don't need to check your pH. However, if your fern appears to be struggling, the pH is one thing to check. You can do this with a simple soil pH test kit. Keep in mind that some species are "lime lovers," preferring a pH of 7 to 8. For these ferns, add a little pulverized limestone to your potting mix when potting the fern. Use dolomitic lime, agricultural limestone, or oyster shells. If you want to sweeten (raise the pH) the mix that a "lime lover" fern is already potted in, try adding touch of baking soda. Other ferns naturally grow in acidic soils or marshy areas and prefer a pH of 4 to 7. If you need to lower the pH (make it more acidic) for these ferns, add a teaspoon of ground sulfur or aluminum sulfate to the potting soil.

Soilless mixes contain no actual soil, hence the name, and are very popular for use in containers. Standard soilless mixes most typically contain peat moss, vermiculite, and perlite. Some might also contain composted bark or coir. Peat moss should not be considered a renewable resource, and its use should be, and in some cases is being, phased out. Renewable coir fiber from coconut husks is a good substitute for peat moss (see page 59 for more on coir fiber). The organic components of soilless mixes   including peat moss, coir, bark, and compost—are mainly responsible for holding the moisture and nutrients. These are mixed with other, inorganic components that improve drainage and aeration, such as vermiculite and perlite. Pumice, lava rock, AxisDE, and horticultural activated charcoal, all in finer grades, are also great inorganic amendments for soilless mixes.

Beginners should start with ready-made, commercial potting mixes, and if needed or desired, customize them accordingly. I usually start with a ready-made mix as my base and then tweak it. Whatever you use, make sure that your growing medium is sterile and "clean." Don't reuse old mixes or dig up soil from outdoors. These may not be in good physical shape, but more important, they could contain pathogens, harmful critters, weed seeds, and other undesirable elements that you don't want to bring indoors.

- **Coir is the thick layer of fibrous material that surrounds coconuts.** A byproduct of processing coconuts, it is a renewable resource and is rapidly gaining popularity. It holds a little more water than peat moss and has a pH closer to desired range.

- **Perlite is volcanic rock that has been subjected to great pressure and very high temperatures** so that the individual particles explode (think popcorn), becoming bigger and lighter with a porous, open structure. These particles don't compress easily under light weight and do not deteriorate rapidly. The coarser (bigger) grades allow for more drainage and aeration, and also do not float or blow away, or rise to the top as easily. Perlite holds a little bit of moisture and has a fair bit of surface area. All particles have a large surface area due to lots of little cracks and crevices. They provide tiny, well-aerated pockets for roots to penetrate and cling to, and potentially absorb water, while getting plenty of oxygen.

- **Vermiculite is another volcanic rock that has undergone basically the same treatment that produces perlite.** Vermiculite particles resemble miniature accordions and hold more moisture and nutrients than perlite. They too have a lot of surface area. Coarser grades don't compress as easily and are better in a potting mix, especially for ferns.

- **Pumice, lava rock, and diatomaceous earth-based products such as AxisDE** in finer grades are excellent additions for improving drainage and aeration. These will not compress nor deteriorate, and they provide tremendous surface area.

- **Horticultural activated charcoal also provides drainage and aeration.** It helps to absorb toxins, prevents your soil from souring, and keeps your pH more stable. I like to add it to just about any of my potting mixes! Charcoal, lava rock, and pumice, depending on how dark the color is, blend in more with the earthy tones of the organic matter and lend a more natural look to your mix than vermiculite or perlite.

◀ Choosing the correct potting mix for your ferns is essential. It must drain well yet hold sufficient moisture and nutrients for ferns to thrive.

◄ Ready-made and home-made potting mixes for ferns can include many different ingredients, such as perlite, vermiculite, peat moss, charcoal, pumice, and other materials.

THREE BASIC RECIPES FOR GROWING FERNS

1. Use a standard potting mix for many species of potted ferns.

2. Use a mix that is lighter, coarser, and more porous for plants that need better drainage. This well-drained fern mix is good for most epiphytic ferns that have smaller, more slender rhizomes, such as *Davallia* species, and most of the epiphytes that you typically grow in the home.

3. Use a very coarse mix for larger epiphytic ferns (plants that grow not in the ground, but up in trees—see Chapter 2). As a general rule for these, the bigger the epiphyte's rhizome, the coarser the medium. This coarse epiphytic fern mix is appropriate for ferns with large, thick rhizomes, in case you want to grow one of these handsome, but often large ferns (e.g., *Aglaomorpha* spp.). In general, epiphytes do well in mossed baskets, but another option for growing some epiphytes is to mount them in various ways using long-fiber sphagnum moss (see Chapter 5 for more information).

When making any of these three mixes, add a dry, granular, organic fertilizer (see "Fertilizing Your Ferns" on page 71).

RECIPE 1 | STANDARD FERN MIX

Use it for most species of container-grown ferns.

➤ One part organic component: coir, peat moss, compost, or any combination of these. You can also use most brand-name standard soilless potting mixes.

➤ One part inorganic component for drainage: perlite, vermiculite, pumice, lava rock, AxisDE, or a combination of these—but try not to use vermiculite alone.

➤ Add 1 tablespoon of horticultural activated charcoal for each quart (liter) of finished mix.

Moss baskets are great for some epiphytic "footed" ferns with smaller rhizomes. Notice their rhizomes beginning to creep over the sides of the baskets. Left front: *Davallia tyermanii*. Rear, left to right: *Polypodium formosanum*, *Phlebodium aureum* 'Blue Star', *Microsorum pustulatum*.

RECIPE 2 | WELL-DRAINED FERN MIX

Use it for potted ferns needing more drainage, and for epiphytes with smaller rhizomes.

- One part organic component: coir, peat moss, compost, or any combination of these. You can also use most brand-name standard soilless potting mixes.

- One and a half parts inorganic components for drainage: perlite, vermiculite, pumice, lava rock, AxisDE, or a combination of these—but try not to use more than one part vermiculite.

- Add 1 tablespoon of horticultural activated charcoal for each quart (liter) of the finished mix.

RECIPE 3 | COARSE EPIPHYTIC FERN MIX

Use it for epiphytes with larger rhizomes.

- One part organic component: coir, peat moss, compost, or any combination of these. You can also use most brand-name standard soilless potting mixes.

- One part ready-made orchid mix containing fir bark, charcoal, and coarse perlite.

WATERING

The importance of proper watering cannot be stressed enough. Improper watering is a leading cause of death for houseplants. It is very common for people to overwater their houseplants, "killing them with kindness" or "loving them to death." Proper watering isn't very hard to learn, but you must first understand the basic concepts. Watering is intimately connected with the growing medium. If your potting mix holds too much water for the type of fern you are growing, the roots might begin to rot even if you don't water frequently. You can begin to understand now how the proper medium can help you water your ferns properly. Always check your fern's preferences to know how much water it requires. In general, most indoor ferns come from tropical habitats, particularly moist, tropical forests, where there is ample moisture and ample humidity. These ferns generally prefer to be kept evenly moist. Some ferns, however, come from drier habitats and prefer to be on the slightly dry side. Others might want to be kept on the wet side or may actually be aquatic and need to grow in water.

Watering depends not only on the type of fern you're growing and the potting mix the plant is growing in, but also on the size of the container and whether the container is plastic or clay (clay is porous and dries out a lot faster). Other factors include how warm it is, how much light the plant is receiving, the humidity levels, and air movement. It should be easy to see why there is no single rule about how much to water and how frequently to do it. The best approach is to check each plant daily and water when needed. If you have a plant for a long time, you'll get to know it, and you'll have a better idea of what to expect.

▶ Water ferns from the top, allowing excess water to drain out the hole in the bottom of the pot. If the pot has a saucer, be sure to pour away any water that collects in it.

How to Water

When you water, it's best to use water at room temperature. Water that is too cold or too hot can be shocking, even damaging, to your ferns. If possible, collect rainwater and use it for all your houseplants. Fluoride and chlorine are often added to tap water, but the amounts are usually not harmful to ferns. However, it doesn't hurt to fill jugs and let them sit for twenty-four hours, uncovered, to let the chlorine dissipate out (people who have fish tanks are familiar with this process). If your water source is softened, you should avoid using it because the sodium in the water is not good for the plants or the soil. You can recycle water from the basin of your dehumidifier, or if you've boiled some plain vegetables, save the water to water your plants—just make sure it has cooled down first.

When you're growing a fern in a container with potting mix, the container should have one or more drainage holes. This allows you to water the plant thoroughly, from top to bottom, allowing the excess water to escape through the drainage hole(s). If your container is sitting in a saucer, make sure to empty the saucer if any water remains a half hour after watering. When watering, don't pour the water over the top of your fern, wetting all the foliage. The idea is to water the soil where the roots are but keep the foliage dry. Apply water at the soil line and distribute it evenly all the way around—water moves down, not sideways. If you have to add water a few times before it comes out the bottom, do so.

Another option is to water from beneath, filling the saucer and letting the potting mix and roots draw up the water like a wick. Make sure that the saucer has enough water to moisten the soil all the way up to the top of the pot. Refill the saucer as necessary until no more water is absorbed, then pour out the excess.

Alternatively (and efficiently), you can plunge the pot into a container of water up to the top rim of the pot and let it soak for a few minutes. Then remove the pot and let it drain fully.

If you have ferns that are not potted, but mounted onto a slab of wood, cork, or the like, it is best to plunge the entire piece in a bucket of water and let it soak for 5 to 10 minutes. Remove the mounted fern, let it drip dry, and put it back on display. You can also give it a shower—literally—for a couple of minutes and let it drip dry.

When to Water

Now that you understand how to water, the question is *when* to water. Periodically, lift your container and feel how heavy it is just after watering. Also lift it a few days later to see what it feels like when it is beginning to dry out. For unglazed clay pots, practice tapping on the side of the pot with your knuckles. If it is very dry, it will make a hollow ringing sound. If it is very wet, it will sound more like a thud. For most ferns that like to be kept evenly moist, wait until the soil is dry on the surface before watering. Lift the pot to gauge how wet or dry it is, and if it is a clay pot, give it a tap. Use all these things to help you decide when it's time to water, and don't forget to look at the plant itself. Don't wait until a fern is so dry that it's wilting. Most ferns are not forgiving, and those wilted and dried fronds will not revive. Forgiving ferns are the exception, not the rule. For those select ferns that prefer to be on the dry side, let them go a little longer. Stick your finger about ¼ to ½ inch (6 to 13 mm) down into the soil—if it's dry, it's time to water. Again, use all the little tricks you have at your disposal to gauge just how dry the soil is. The easiest watering chores to manage are for ferns that like to be wet. If the soil isn't completely moist to wet on the surface, it's time to water. Remember, no matter what the ferns' preference is, when it is time to water, water thoroughly, until the excess water comes out the bottom.

Dormancy

Many types of plants have a dormant phase, and ferns are no exception. A few ferns may go partially or completely dormant during the winter months, though this can sometimes depend on the environment they're growing in. Some species of *Davallia* (rabbit's foot fern), might shed most of their fronds briefly in the winter as they rest, or they might shed old fronds as new ones are unfurling. Any time your plant has shed its leaves in a restful state, or it has been subjected to some stressful condition that has left it with very little foliage growth, be much more sparing with your water. Without leaves, your fern needs much less water. You don't want to overwater and kill your plant while it's in the resting phase. When you see your fern making new fiddleheads and resuming growth, resume watering carefully—a little growth, a little water, more growth, more water.

HUMIDITY

Humidity is an important consideration when growing ferns—in particular relative humidity, which is the relationship between the temperature and humidity. If the relative humidity is 50 percent, it means that the air is holding only half the amount of water that the air can hold at that temperature. The warmer the air, the more moisture it can hold, so as the temperature goes up, it requires more water in the air to maintain the "same" level of humidity. For example, the amount of water vapor in the air at 65°F (18°C) with a relative humidity of 50 percent would be less than the amount of water vapor in the air at 75°F (24°C) with a relative humidity of 50 percent.

As you now know, most of the ferns we grow indoors come from moist tropical forests, where the humidity is typically 70 to 90 percent. Some ferns live in areas with constant 100 percent humidity.

(continued on page 70)

Signs that it's time to water your fern include wilted fronds, a light pot, and soil that's dry to the touch.

SPECIALIZED POTTING TECHNIQUES THAT AID IN WATERING

SELF-WATERING POTS

Self-watering pots are available in a variety of styles, sizes, and materials. They basically consist of a pot-in-pot system with a water reservoir inside. In a properly designed pot, the soil draws water up from the reservoir as the plant needs it. Consistent watering in such a way is much healthier for your ferns and reduces extreme fluctuations in soil moisture and the likelihood of over- or underwatering. A self-watering pot with a built-in water reservoir typically needs to be topped off with water less frequently, making it easier for the gardener as well. The outer container is decorative, hiding the inner workings while housing the water reservoir.

With plastic versions, the inner container has a specially shaped base, narrowed at the bottom, with openings designed to sit in the reservoir and draw water up from it, while keeping the rootball of the plant above the waterline of the reservoir. Clay versions are very popular among African violet growers. With these, the outer pot is usually glazed to make it watertight, while the inner pot is unglazed. With either plastic or clay self-watering containers, as the potting mix dries out, it draws just enough water from the reservoir to maintain the ideal soil moisture level. You'll need to check and refill the water reservoir on a regular basis, but for people who can't check their plants daily, or tend to forget to water, self-watering pots can be extremely helpful. You can also make your own—however, homemade versions are generally not as aesthetically pleasing.

Water wicks offer another way to provide consistent watering for your ferns and make it easier on yourself. Essentially, you are using a wick to draw water from a basin to create your own self-watering container. For wicking to work well, you need an open, well-aerated potting mix that provides good capillary movement of water. The potting mixes listed on page 60 will work well. However, the coarse epiphytic mix will not have very good capillary action.

Wicking is more effective with plastic or glazed ceramic pots. Wicking can be used with terracotta or wooden pots, but because these are porous materials, water will continually be wicked away from the soil and out into the air via evaporation.

Wicking can also be a great help with very small pots that tend to need frequent attention. Your fern pot sits on top of the water basin or down inside the rim of the water basin, but the bottom of your fern pot must always stay above the waterline. Repurpose a glass or plastic container, such as a glass jar or plastic deli container, to serve as the water basin. Then create a wick to run from the water basin up into the base of your fern pot.

▶ This pair of photographs shares the basic materials and steps needed to make your own wicking system to water plants. A wick is inserted through the bottom of the pot. One end of the wick rests against the potting soil in the pot, and the other end sits in a reservoir of water in the bottom of a glass vessel. As the soil dries out, water is wicked from the reservoir up to the plant.

TIPS FOR SETTING UP A WICKING SYSTEM

→ Natural fibers, such as cotton, tend to collect fungi and bacteria and will rot in time.

→ Thick synthetic fibers, such as acrylic, nylon, and polyester, are usually preferred.

→ Soak the wicking fibers in water before using them, and make sure that your plant is thoroughly watered before setting up the wicking system.

→ The smaller the pot, the thinner the wicking material can be.

→ Test your wick first to make sure it works. Soak it in water, and then, leaving one end in the water, bring the other end up to a dry piece of paper and lay it on the surface. Wait a little while (an hour or more) and see if the paper is soaking up water. If it is, your wicking material is working. If not, select a different wicking material.

→ The bigger the pot, the more wicks it will need. Pots 3 inches (7.6 cm) across or smaller should be fine with a single wick, 6-inch (15 cm) pots should have two or possibly three wicks, and so on. Make sure the wicks are distributed evenly around the rootball and that they touch the soil inside the pot.

→ It's easiest to add wicks up through the bottom drainage holes and into the soil when you're potting your ferns, rather than doing it after they've already been planted.

→ For established plants, place wicks in the soil from the top, instead of going up through the bottom drainage hole(s). Insert the wicks into the top of the potting mix, and use a pencil, screwdriver, or crochet hook to push them all the way down through the soil and out the drainage holes. Use care—you don't want to damage the roots.

→ Once your wicks are in place, they will dangle out the drainage holes. One end remains in contact with the soil, while the other is coiled around the bottom of the water basin below. The basin needs to be near the fern pot because wicking becomes very sluggish if the water travels more than 8 to 10 inches (20 to 25 cm). Check periodically to make sure that the basin is filled with water. As long as there's water in the basin, the wick will draw it upward and into the soil.

DOUBLE POTTING

Double potting is a technique that is used to maintain consistent moisture levels in the container, provide some additional humidity, and help reduce fluctuations in soil temperature and air exchange. It is especially helpful with finicky plants. Most *Adiantum* species need well-drained, aerated soils and cannot stand too much water. However, they are also unforgiving if they get too dry. Like Goldilocks, they need everything just right! If you're not going to put them in a terrarium, try double potting them.

To double pot, plant your fern in a terracotta pot that is porous and allows for good air exchange around the root system. Nestle this pot into a slightly larger, nonporous pot, making sure that both pots have drainage holes. Fill the space between your potted fern and the outer pot completely with fine sand, potting mix, or uncut sphagnum moss (long-fiber sphagnum moss). I generally prefer sand because it is the best aerated and most well-drained, it doesn't break down, and it's effective. The fern's pot

should be surrounded by, and level with, the top of the sand between the pots. Water the inner pot with your fern as needed and keep the sand moist. This technique is also particularly helpful with very small pots, which don't have much of a margin for error when it comes to watering. Many indoor ferns are not finicky and don't need to be double potted, but they would be very happy with the extra effort.

VACATION WATERING

If you're going on vacation for up to 10 days, make sure all your ferns are watered before you leave. Group them together in the sink or bathtub, or cover each plant with a big, clear plastic bag, to slow down their water usage and loss. (Make sure they don't receive any bright, direct light while they're enclosed in the clear plastic bags or they could get "fried"!) Putting the ferns in a location with less light and possibly even slightly cooler temperatures will also help to slow moisture loss for short periods of time. Do a trial run before you leave to see how well your plants handle everything. If your trial run doesn't work perfectly, you might consider installing wicks, or asking a family member or friend to come over and check your plants while you are away.

▲ Double potting, done here with *Adiantum macrophyllum*, is a great way to maintain consistent moisture levels in the potting medium.

Pebble trays offer a great way to raise the humidity level around ferns. Fill a tray with pebbles and add water. The pot sits above the water level, but as the water evaporates from the tray, it increases the humidity. Left to right: *Pteris cretica* 'Mayii', *Asplenium antiquum* 'Crissie', *Hemionitis arifolia*.

Ferns that grow in these super-humid environments do not adapt well to a home environment. You might be able to grow them in a terrarium, but not out in the open. The best ferns for growing indoors are those adapted to slightly drier conditions in their natural settings, making them more tolerant and better suited to an indoor setting. These include ferns from tropical forests that experience some seasonal dry periods and don't receive consistent rainfall. They typically grow on rocks or are epiphytic and grow in trees.

In temperate climates, cold winter air is already dry, and when you heat the indoor environment, it becomes even drier. Such a heated home typically

falls in the range of 10 to 30 percent humidity in winter, the same range as deserts! This is not only difficult for many types of plants, but for humans as well. For our health, humidity should be between 35 and 65 percent. Dry air damages our mucous membranes and makes us more susceptible to bacterial infections, colds, allergies, and asthma. The average summer humidity in a temperate climate ranges from 40 to 60 percent. This is good for us and for many plants, although air conditioning can also dry out the air during the summer months. While the great majority of ferns thrive in humidity between 60 and 80 percent, many of the commonly grown indoor ferns will do fine with humidity levels between 40 and

60 percent. This is usually not hard to achieve during spring, summer, and fall in a temperate climate, but you can see how winter changes everything. I do have some good news for you, though! The following tips help raise humidity levels around ferns and other houseplants.

Tips for increasing the relative humidity:

➺ Get a humidifier. It's a great solution, not only for the plants, but for you as well. Make sure to locate the humidifier where the humidity reaches your ferns.

➺ Group your ferns together. The more plants you gather together, the greater the humidity in their immediate vicinity.

➺ Use humidity trays. Put your ferns on trays or saucers filled with pebbles (or covered with a plastic grate). Add water to the tray or saucer so that the bottoms of your pots do not sit in the water, but rather sit above it. This humidifies the air around the plants.

➺ Combine strategies. Grouping ferns on pebble trays is even better because it puts both strategies to work for you.

➺ Use the kitchen and bath. If you have enough light, growing ferns in the bathroom or kitchen provides them with some extra humidity from human activities.

➺ Use double potting. Double potting (described earlier) can also be helpful to increase humidity for an individual fern.

➺ Use a terrarium. Ferns that require very high humidity are better kept in a terrarium. Terrariums are a very fun way to grow ferns with high humidity requirements (see Chapter 5 for a terrarium-planting lesson).

What doesn't raise the humidity? Misting and overwatering. Lightly misting your ferns won't do much to change the humidity because as soon as the water dries, the humidity is gone. Misting ferns often enough to maintain sufficient humidity keeps the fronds wet too much of the time, and that can lead to other negative issues, including rot. It is better to raise the humidity around the plants without wetting the plants themselves. Some people also make the mistake of thinking that constantly wet soil will make up for a lack of humidity. This is absolutely *not* the case. You will just overwater the fern and kill it. For the most part, the ferns profiled later in this chapter tolerate the humidity of a typical indoor home environment, unless otherwise noted.

FERTILIZING YOUR FERNS

Ferns, like all green plants, require mineral nutrients to grow. Growing ferns in containers indoors is completely different than growing them outdoors in their native habitats. With a limited amount of potting mix, the nutrient supply is eventually depleted. Proper fertilization is necessary for any containerized plant to keep the nutrients at levels sufficient for healthy growth. In general, if your fern is making normal, green growth, you probably don't need to fertilize, unless you're trying to make your fern grow bigger or faster. But if growth slows or the plant begins to yellow, it's time to start a fertilizer regimen.

Choosing a Fertilizer

All fertilizers state the percentages of the three primary macronutrients found in them on their label. This is called the N-P-K ratio. For example, a label with 4-3-3 lets you know that 4 percent of that bag or bottle is nitrogen (N), 3 percent is phosphorus (P), and 3 percent is potassium (K).

Organic fertilizers are derived from organic substances, whereas inorganic, synthetic fertilizers are chemically derived and often salt based. Organic fertilizers generally have a low N-P-K ratio; if you add all three numbers together, they usually don't go

◂ Organic, granular fertilizers are safe bets for ferns and other houseplants. Add them to the potting mix when repotting or add a very small amount to the pot every few months from spring until fall.

higher than 15. Organic fertilizers, like those based on fish and kelp (seaweed), will not burn your ferns. They are great choices. Plus, they're better for the environment. Ferns are sensitive to overfertilizing, and this is just one reason why I prefer organic fertilizers. Synthetic (inorganic) fertilizers can also do the job well, but it's important to find one with a lower N-P-K ratio to keep from "burning" your fern.

Whichever you choose, get a complete fertilizer (one with all three primary macronutrients present) that is balanced. Fertilizers are available in different forms, including liquid, water-soluble powder, and dry granules. With potted indoor ferns, I find it easiest to use liquid fertilizers as I water. If you're doing some repotting, add a granular organic fertilizer to your potting mix. This provides enough nutrients for the first two months, possibly longer. When you purchase a new fern from a reputable source, the potting mix likely already contains fertilizer. There is no easy way to know for sure, but on average, you should expect it to last a month or two. Keep an eye on your fern to see if it's happy and healthy, and if you think it isn't looking quite as good as it should, check the Troubleshooting Guide beginning on page 78.

How Much and How Often to Fertilize Ferns

Never fertilize a fern that is wilted or whose potting mix is very dry. First water the fern in its pot, then wait a day for it to recover before fertilizing. When using an organic, liquid fish and kelp fertilizer, or another water-soluble fertilizer, mix it at half the recommended strength. For example, if the label says add 1 teaspoon per gallon (5 ml per 3.8 L) of water, mix only ½ teaspoon per gallon (2.5 ml per 3.8 L) of water. If your ferns are in a less-than-ideal setting and don't ever make a lot of growth, you can lower the

rate to one-quarter strength. Do this once a month during the growing season, basically from the beginning of spring until the beginning of fall. Where I live, in New York, the first dose of the season is on March 1 and the last is on October 1.

In areas where the winter months mean short days and low light intensity, ferns are in a holding pattern, resting. Do not fertilize ferns during this time. Fertilizing ferns in the winter only promotes growth that is not capable of developing properly under such poor conditions. Give them their rest and let the growth cycle start over again in spring.

If you live near the equator and have year-round growing conditions, go ahead and fertilize every month, all year long. All too often, people overfertilize with the intention of helping their ferns. Resist the urge—too much is not a good thing. You might hear of growers fertilizing more frequently and with higher concentrations than I recommend here, but realize that they are most often experienced professionals, in the business of producing plants, and they have it down to a science. Literally.

DAILY FERN CARE

Plants growing in our homes are dependent on us for their care and well-being. Have a look at your ferns regularly, ideally every day, and you will get to know them very well. Do they look happy and healthy? When checking to see if they need water, give them a quick inspection. Do you notice anything different? Bumps, spots, stickiness, and brown edges or tips are often signs of pests or cultural problems. Good plant hygiene is important. Remove dead, diseased, infested, or otherwise unhealthy growth to help keep problems in check. It's normal for an occasional, old frond to turn yellow. If possible, wait to remove yellow leaves until they've browned, as they still hold food and it takes a little time for the food to be transported out of the dying frond and into the rest of the plant. Once fronds are dry and brown it is not only safe, but in most cases desirable to remove them. If

they don't fall away cleanly, cut them off, close to the base, using clean, sharp shears.

Ferns also benefit from regular grooming to keep them looking their best. If dust accumulates on their fronds, delicately dust them off or give them a gentle shower. If weeds should ever sprout up in your pots, be sure to remove them. Pay attention to the potting mix as well. When you water, does the water sit on the surface and slowly soak in, or has the mix shrunk in from the pot edges and the water just runs down the sides? Do you see a white, crusty layer on the soil or on the container? These are conditions that should be addressed according to the suggestions in the Troubleshooting Guide on page 78. Signs of new spring growth, especially if coupled with stronger light and warmer temperatures, are indications to slowly increase watering, fertilizing, and repotting, if necessary. Low light levels (typical of winter) and/or cooler temperatures are conditions that warrant reduced watering and fertilizing. Observation and showing your ferns a little love keeps them thriving.

POTTING INDOOR FERNS

When you "pot on," or "pot up," it means that you're transplanting your plant into a larger pot. The general rule is to move up one pot size at a time. If your plant is in a 4-inch (10 cm) pot, the next size would be a 5- or 6-inch (13 to 15 cm) pot. A typical progression would be from a 2-inch (5 cm) pot to a 4-inch (10 cm) pot, a 4-inch (10 cm) to a 6-inch (15 cm) pot, a 6-inch (15 cm) to an 8-inch (20 cm) pot, and so on. Think of it this way: When you're a toddler, you wear tiny sneakers, not adult-size shoes, and your feet grow larger slowly, not overnight. Don't overpot by jumping from a 4-inch (10 cm) pot to a 10-inch (25 cm) pot. It won't save time, and it could even kill your fern because the potting mix will stay too wet, rotting roots and even turning sour. "Repotting" is another term you may hear. This means you are taking the plant out of its container, brushing off a little of the old soil, cleaning your pot, or getting a new one of the same size, and putting the plant back into the container with some fresh soil, but *not* moving it up in pot size.

◀ Trim old or dead fronds from ferns soon after they brown, using a clean pair of shears.

▶ Plant pots come in many different sizes. When potting up a plant, move up just one pot size at a time.

Signs You Need to Pot Up Your Fern

Ideally, your potting mix should be loose enough on the surface to allow water to percolate down through it quickly. When you water your fern, if the water sits on the surface, taking a long time to percolate down through the potting mix, it is usually an indication that the structure of your mix has deteriorated, and it needs to be replaced. Alternatively, if your fern has filled its pot with roots (this is called rootbound or potbound), it's time to move up to the next pot size. Moving your fern into a slightly larger pot gives the roots the space and moisture they need to grow bigger. Crowded roots leave very little space for water. If you find yourself watering constantly and still not getting the best results, it's time to pot up the plant. Another sign that it might be best to change your potting mix is when you see the potting soil shrinking and pulling away from the pot. In this case, water simply runs across the top and down the outside, never soaking into the root zone. This is a particularly common problem with mixes containing a lot of peat moss.

When to Pot Up Your Fern

The time to repot or pot up is late winter or early spring, just as the growing season begins. Signs of new growth will let you know the fern is ready. Don't repot or pot up a fern when it is entering a resting phase, such as in the fall. Potting up and repotting require the fern to make new growth in order to establish itself in its new home. You don't want to encourage your fern to grow when conditions are not conducive to healthy growth. This will not only produce poor growth but also strain the fern's stored energy supply. Allow your fern to use its food stores to help sustain itself while it rests.

What Kind of Pot to Use

Pots are made of different materials. Choose from plastic, clay, wood, metal, fiberglass, fabric, and even recycled paper. Plastic and clay are the most commonly available. Plastic doesn't breathe and so it will hold water longer and not dry out as quickly. Many ferns that like to be moister, and don't need as much

There are many different types and
styles of pots available for growing
ferns. Be sure to choose one that
suits your décor. Just make sure it has
a drainage hole in the bottom.

air around their roots, benefit from being in plastic. Clay is porous and allows for good air circulation around the root zone but will dry out more quickly because of this. Choose the type of container you think is best, based on the fern's preferences and your environmental conditions.

Whatever container you choose, make sure it has a drainage hole. Many decorative containers do not have drainage holes. If you want to use one, pot your fern in an appropriate container with a drainage hole, and then set the pot inside the decorative one. Otherwise, find a way to open a drainage hole (there are special drill bits for clay pottery). Without drainage, you risk suffocating the roots, and are likely to kill your fern.

Feel free to get creative with containers. If they provide adequate drainage and are nontoxic, all sorts of decorative holders become possibilities. Take a moment to see if there are any items than can be repurposed, perhaps an old Tonka toy truck or candle holders—you'll be surprised at what you find when you start looking! There are also many gorgeous and interesting ways to plant your house ferns without using traditional containers. See the Chapter 5 for some fun ideas.

◀ Repotting ferns into a larger size pot is essential to keep them happy and healthy. The process isn't difficult.

STEP 1: Cover the drainage hole with a small piece of fiberglass window screening to keep the potting mix from falling out through the drainage hole, but without impeding drainage or aeration. This is helpful, but not necessary.

STEP 2: Place some potting mix in the bottom of your container, just enough to reach the bottom of the rootball of the fern you are going to pot. It's best to tap the fern out of its existing pot so that you can check exactly how much potting mix to put in. To take the fern out of its pot, spread your pointer and middle fingers apart and place them gently over the top of the pot, with the fern between your fingers. Next, invert the pot and tap the bottom of the pot until the fern slides out.

STEP 3: Gently loosen the old potting mix from around the outside, top, and bottom of the rootball, allowing the tips of the roots to be exposed. Once ready, place the fern into the pot, on top of the soil, making sure the top of the rootball sits just below the top rim of the new pot.

The Best Technique for Repotting or Potting Up Ferns

When you're planning to pot up or repot, it's a good idea to water your fern well the day before. This ensures that excess water has time to drain away, the rootball is moist, it will come out of the container easily, and it is less likely to be damaged.

Always start with a pot that is perfectly clean when potting. Use a new pot or prepare previously used pots by soaking them in a 10 percent bleach solution (1 part bleach and 9 parts water), scrubbing, thoroughly rinsing, and allowing them to dry. This prevents possible diseases or pests from being carried along the way.

STEP 4: Gently fill in around the rootball with potting mix. For a container that is 4 inches (10 cm) or less, fill it almost up to the top of the soil line of the rootball. Then, using your fingers, press the potting mix gently around the rootball. This will firm it, keep it in place, and help to make good contact between the rootball and the new potting mix, preventing big air pockets. Keep filling around and gently firming until the soil is even with the soil line all around the rootball. Give it a little shake to settle the potting mix and even it out. Make sure that you leave yourself a watering lip. In a small pot like a 4-inch (10 cm) pot, you might want to leave about ½ inch (13 mm) maximum.

STEP 5: After you have your plant at the right level, you've filled it and firmed it, and you have a watering lip, it's time to water it in. This will provide the final settling, putting all the soil in contact with the rootball and eliminating air pockets. It's also a good idea to get in the habit of labeling your plants. With a pencil, write the fern's name and the potting date on a simple plastic label and stick it in the pot. Later, you can add other information, such as when you fertilized, or the date a plant went dormant. We all think we will remember these things, but we don't. Having it all on the label is helpful and easy.

Troubleshooting Guide

We all want our plants to look their best—there is no joy in watching them decline. Many common problems with growing ferns indoors are cultural concerns: too little or too much light, underwatering or overwatering, temperature issues, dry air, and improper fertilizing. Pests and pathogens can also cause trouble for your ferns. If you think your fern is not thriving, use the information provided here to help you determine possible causes. Keep in mind that, in general, young ferns, recently transplanted ones, those that have a lot of new, tender growth, and ferns that are weak or stressed are in a more vulnerable state. These ferns are more sensitive and can be more easily damaged.

◄ Ferns require sufficient light levels to encourage new growth, but not so much that their foliage is scorched.

Cultural Concerns

Light Issues

Symptoms of insufficient light include no new growth (particularly during the growing season); smaller than normal growth; pale fronds; weak, thin, spindly growth; and growth leaning heavily toward the light. Signs of too much light are foliage wilting during the sunny hours of the day (especially if the potting mix is moist); smaller, stunted, less luxuriant fronds; leaves with a yellowish-green color; and/or browning on the leaf edges. In extreme situations, you may see brown patches from scorching, or a kind of bleached look, which produces a whitish, washed-out, ghost-like color.

Water Issues

Underwatering: When a fern doesn't get enough water, the fronds often develop dry, brown edges, and new or young tender growth shrivels and dries up. Ferns with a softer texture will have mature fronds wilt and dry. Species whose fronds have a thicker texture that don't wilt easily may curl a bit. Some may even temporarily turn a paler shade. Most ferns are not very forgiving, and severely water-stressed fronds shrivel and dry within days. Dead fronds should be removed as soon as possible. If you find your fern is wilted, or exhibiting any of the signs just mentioned, and it is dry, immediately immerse the entire pot in a bucket of water. In severe cases, plunge the entire plant, fronds and all, into the bucket. When it is thoroughly soaked and has stopped bubbling (this is all the air bubbling out as it is being replaced by water) remove it from the bucket and let it drain. If possible, put the fern in a shaded, slightly cooler location until it recovers.

Overwatering: Too frequent, or too much, water causes new and young growth to simply collapse or get mushy. Green fronds fall off, especially if it's a sudden and severe condition, or fronds might turn yellow before falling off in a less severe condition. In extreme overwatering conditions, ferns wilt and collapse, and the potting mix may even smell foul due to being waterlogged.

When a plant is overwatered, it is not that the plant is getting too much water, but rather that the roots are being deprived of oxygen. The water forces the air out of the soil and suffocates the roots. The roots rot and die. If your fern has been overwatered, tap it out of its pot to determine how badly the root system and rhizomes have been damaged. If the root system is basically in good shape, reduce your watering and monitor very carefully. If there is some damage, trim away the rotted roots and repot using a fresh, well-drained potting mix, and be careful with watering in the future. If your fern has already wilted from severe overwatering, and you find that the root system is mainly rotten, it is probably best to discard the fern. Excess water from overwatering also promotes bacterial and fungal diseases, which can do additional harm to your fern.

Temperature Issues

Extreme temperatures also negatively impact your ferns. Too much warmth pushes your fern into rapid growth, causing thin, spindly, and stretched fronds. During the low-light days of winter, this is often due to too much heat coupled with not enough light, which is why it is best to keep your ferns a little cooler and drier during this time so that all the cultural factors are more balanced. Thin, spindly growth when there is ample light, such as during the growing season, is most likely a sign that the plant needs fertilizer. Extremely high temperatures could also scorch your fern fronds.

Temperatures cooler than the fern tolerates cause new and young growth to turn black, become mushy, and collapse. Other symptoms are possible lesions on the frond surface that are discolored and/or water-soaked. If low enough, temperatures can also cause the whole fern to become droopy. If cool temperatures are extreme enough, ferns not suited to such

conditions might survive, but they will let you know how unhappy they are, with most growth yellowing and dying, making little, if any new growth and being very slow to recover. If the situation is severe enough, the fern will slowly waste away. Ferns also resent wide fluctuations in temperature. The greater—and quicker—the change, the worse it is for the fern. Drafts are also not good for ferns, as they usually cause extreme temperature fluctuations and have a drying effect.

Humidity Issues

Dry air is a common problem when growing ferns indoors, especially during the winter season. Generally speaking, ferns with thin-textured fronds (for example, maidenhair ferns, *Adiantum* spp.) prefer more humidity, while ferns whose fronds are thicker and feel leathery, or even a little like plastic, are more tolerant of lower humidity (for example, *Arachniodes simplicior* and *Microsorum punctatum*). Signs that the humidity is too low for your fern are drying and browning on the tips and/or the edges of the fronds.

Drying and shriveling of developing new growth is also a common sign, as is the yellowing and fading of older fronds sooner than normal.

Pay close attention to hot, dry air blowing out of heating ducts during cold weather—this can be devastating to plants in general. Humid indoor air might be found in the tropics or during the warm months in temperate regions, but this is rarely a concern for plants, especially for ferns, which tend to like higher humidity. Typically, you would see overly humid conditions only inside a terrarium, and then only if the terrarium is on the wet side. Most terrariums should not be kept so wet that they have heavy condensation collecting on the inner surface of the lid and dropping onto the ferns. Small drops of water on the sides of the glass that don't fall like rain are fine. Whatever the situation, if the fronds are always wet and experiencing constant humidity with no air circulation, problems are likely to develop. You may see moist, brown patches on the fronds, which eventually disintegrate. You may see gray, even fuzzy, spots forming on the fronds, which are signs of a fungal infection.

◀ Placing ferns in kitchens and bathrooms is a great idea because these rooms are often slightly more humid than other parts of the house.

▶ The white crust on the outside of these empty clay pots is due to the buildup of fertilizer salts. If you see this occurring on your fern pots, it's time to act.

And you may even see algae growing on the fronds and/or on the inside surface of the container. If algae are growing on the glass, it blocks light from entering the terrarium. If algae are growing on the fronds, it blocks light from entering the leaf.

Fertilizer Issues

Maintaining suitable nutrient levels in your potting mix helps your fern to thrive. During the growing season, if your fern is growing more slowly, is smaller than usual, is not looking quite as green as it should, or is making fronds of lesser quality, your potting mix is likely lacking nutrients. Begin to supplement with a water-soluble fertilizer.

Too much fertilizer can cause dry, brown edges on your fronds and push weak, lanky growth during winter. A single, strong dose is enough to severely burn your fern, or even kill it. If you notice a white, crusty layer forming on the surface of your potting mix or the inside or outside of your container, take action. This is often the result of overfertilization and/or of using inorganic, salt-based fertilizers. It can also be due to the fact that you are not watering thoroughly enough to leach the excess salts out through the drainage hole. Occasionally salt buildup can be related to the quality of your water (See "Watering," on

POSSIBLE SOLUTIONS FOR OVERWATERING

➳ Decrease the amount and/or frequency of watering.

➳ Use a coarser potting mix that has better drainage and aeration.

➳ Use a porous clay pot instead of a nonporous plastic pot.

➳ Take care not to overpot your fern.

page 62). If the crust is on the surface of the potting mix, but the mix is otherwise in good condition, hold the fern in place, turn the pot over, carefully scrape off all the crust, and then water thoroughly. If the mix needs replacing, unpot your fern, scrape off the crust, and pot with fresh mix as needed. If the crust is on your container, repot into a new pot or temporarily remove the fern from its pot so that the pot can be cleaned. Scrape the crust off the pot, soak it in warm water, give it a good brushing, and rinse it. Vinegar may help dissolve some of the salt but do *not* get

(continue on page 84)

SYMPTOM GUIDE
AND PROBABLE CAUSES

Keep in mind that plant tissue that has died, such as brown tips or spots on the fronds, or shriveled or distorted growth, cannot be reversed. This chart includes some of the most common symptoms of an ailing fern and what to do about them.

SYMPTOMS	CAUSE	SOLUTION
FRONDS WITH BROWN TIPS.	Dry air, physical damage (for example, frond tip pressed against window or wall), drafts	Relocate the plant to a more appropriate site.
FRONDS WITH BROWN MARGINS OR EDGES.	Too much heat (brown, damaged areas where frond was exposed to heat source), underwatering, too much light, possible burn from excessive fertilizer, chemical sprays, or use of water with a high salt content	Reduce fertilization and flush water through pot when watering. Relocate to a more appropriate site if the plant is near a heat source.
FRONDS TURN YELLOW AND FALL OFF OR COLLAPSE.	It is normal for an occasional, older frond to yellow and die. When several do this simultaneously, it could mean trouble. Possible causes include overwatering, too cold, drafts, and natural dormancy.	If it's not the correct time for your fern to shift into a natural dormancy, ensure your fern isn't in a drafty location and that you're not overwatering.
FRONDS SHOW SPOTS OR PATCHES.	If spots are dry and brown, underwatering is the cause. If they're soft and dark brown, overwatering or water sitting on the fronds is to blame. If the spots are white or straw-colored, the plant may be exposed to too much sun. Moist and blisterlike spots, or those that are dry and sunken, could be signs of disease.	Take appropriate action based on the types of spots or patches present. This could mean a change in watering habits, relocation to a site with lower light, or an investigation for the presence of a disease (see Pest and Pathogen Concerns on page 84).
FRONDS ARE YELLOWISH OR ABNORMALLY PALE OR LIGHT GREEN.	Too much light, or not enough fertilizer	Make sure your fern isn't receiving too much sun. If you haven't fertilized in a while, be sure to follow the fertilizer recommendations outlined earlier in this chapter and set up a fertilizer schedule.
FERNS SHOW SHRIVELED, DRY NEW GROWTH.	Underwatering, dry air, or drafts	If new fronds are drying, increase the humidity by placing the fern on a pebble tray. Make sure it's away from heating vents and drafts and keep the plant regularly watered.

SYMPTOMS	CAUSE	SOLUTION
FRONDS SHOW GOOD COLOR AND ARE AMPLE IN SIZE, BUT ALSO THIN AND SOFT.	Too much nitrogen (fertilizer) or too much humidity	Fertilizers that are high in nitrogen (the first number on the package) cause the production of tender new growth. Too much nitrogen makes soft, pest-prone fronds. Reduce fertilization for a few months.
FRONDS HAVE THEIR MARGINS CUPPED UNDER OR OTHERWISE DISTORTED.	Dryness while fronds were developing, insect damage or damage from chemical sprays, or exposure to harmful gases. Air pollutants such as ethylene, carbon monoxide, and sulfur dioxide can injure ferns and other plants. In ferns, the fronds typically curl under and/or turn yellow.	Ripening fruit emits ethylene gas, so do not keep a bowl of fruit next to your fern plants. Make sure the plant is amply watered, check for a possible pest infestation, and limit the plant's exposure to potentially harmful air pollutants.
FRONDS ARE WILTING.	Underwatering, overwatering, too much light, too much heat, dry air, rootbound plant, or overfertilizing	Make sure the drainage holes in the pot are not blocked. If wilting coincides with a sunny time of day and the soil is still moist, the plant may be receiving too much light. Reduce exposure to dry air. Check to make sure the plant is not rootbound and in need of potting up.
FRONDS ARE ROTTING (USUALLY VERY DARK IN COLOR AND SOFT OR MUSHY).	Too much cold, overwatering, or the fronds are wet for extended periods of time, especially overnight	Constant overwatering promotes disease. Keep foliage dry when watering, and don't overwater.
FRONDS SUDDENLY FALL OFF OR COLLAPSE.	Sudden and rapid defoliation—without a prior period of wilting, yellowing, or discoloring—indicates culture shock. Most often the cause is a sudden, intense condition, such as extreme heat or cold, severe sunlight, strong drafts, or profound drying of the root zone.	Care for the plant properly and remove any possible intense conditions. Check the fern's environment carefully.
FERN GROWS SLOWLY OR SHOWS NO GROWTH AT ALL.	This is normal during the winter or dormant phase. During the active growing season, it is likely from too little light, not enough fertilizer, overwatering, too little heat, or the plant rootbound.	Pot up the plant into a larger pot, if it's rootbound. Fertilize regularly throughout the growing season and ensure that the plant is receiving the correct levels of light.
FERN GROWTH IS SMALL, PALE, AND SPINDLY.	In winter, the cause is likely too much heat. During the active growing season, it is likely from too little light or not enough fertilizer.	Fertilize regularly throughout the growing season, and ensure your plant receives enough light.

vinegar on the plant, roots, or soil. Make sure vinegar only comes in contact with the pot, and make sure the container gets thoroughly rinsed before reusing.

Total Plant Collapse

There are many possible causes that can account for the death of your fern, but the following extreme conditions are the most common.

- Overwatering—the single biggest killer of potted indoor plants!
- Underwatering (severe dryness).
- Insufficient light.
- Hot, dry air.
- Cold temperatures.
- Extreme sunlight.
- Drafts.

Movement Shock

Any relocation or transplanting causes changes that require adjustments on the part of your fern that could result in reduced growth, yellowing foliage, and the like. This is normal. However, if the change is too abrupt or extreme, your fern can go into deep shock. See "Potting Indoor Ferns" on page 74 for proper techniques to prevent this, and be sure to protect your new ferns when bringing them home. If you are moving ferns around within your home, do so in stages, so that they have at least a few days to adjust to the light, temperature, and humidity levels in their new home.

Pest and Pathogen Concerns

A healthy plant is the first line of defense against pests and diseases. Ferns and other plants are less likely to be attacked when they're happy and healthy. And if they are attacked, healthy plants are better able to defend themselves and recover. This is another reason why proper growing culture is so important. Fortunately, ferns are not bothered by as many pests and pathogens as many other types of plants are. Make regular inspections of your indoor ferns a part of your daily routine. When scouting for potential problems, it is important to look at all parts of the plant. Signs and early symptoms of pests and diseases may not be as easily visible or obvious as some of the signs associated with cultural troubles. Examine the fronds carefully, especially the undersides and any nooks and crannies, and don't forget to look up and down the leaf stalks. If the rhizome is exposed and visible, be sure to check that as well. Inspect the roots too, particularly if you haven't found anything in the upper part of the fern but your plant seems to be suffering. Early detection limits the damage and makes control much easier.

Pests of Ferns

The first step is to identify the problem. Then you can explore methods of control. Here are some of the more common pests of ferns and ways you can help manage them.

Scale insects and **mealybugs** are the two most common pests of indoor ferns. Both these insects have mouthparts that pierce the plant tissue and suck out the sap. This weakens the fern, causes yellowing of the fronds, and can ultimately kill the plant. They also secrete a sugary substance called honeydew, a type of scale that makes the plants sticky to the touch and is an obvious sign of infestation. If left unchecked, the honeydew in turn provides food for sooty mold, a fungus that grows into a black coating on the fronds. Initially, this doesn't harm the fern, but it will eventually block light from the fronds and thereby reduce or prevent photosynthesis. It is also unattractive.

Both scale insects and mealybugs are adept at reproducing and can get out of control quickly. If the infestation is severe, it's best to dispose of the fern. Scale insects can be white or brown, and covered with a soft or hard shell. They often appear as dots or bumps, particularly on the undersides of the fronds, along the veins, sometimes on the upper surfaces, and up and down the stipes, or frond stalks. Most people find scale insects hard to detect—they're easily confused with sori (the clusters containing the spores—see Chapter 2). Scale insects are difficult to wash off the plants, but it's easy to dab them off with a cotton swab dipped in rubbing alcohol. Mealybugs look like little white cottony masses and are usually easier to recognize. Other species of mealybug attack the root system, so tap your fern out of its pot and look for the white, cottony masses on the roots, too. On fronds, wash off mealybugs or dab them off with a cotton swab dipped in rubbing alcohol. Wash them off roots, and if they are badly infested, gently wash off all soil and replant the fern into fresh growing medium.

Aphids are not common on ferns, especially those grown indoors, but they do like the soft, tender growth. When aphids feed on the developing growth, they cause distortion and stunting of the fronds. These insects have the same mode of feeding as scale insects and mealybugs—they suck juices from the plant using a piercing and sucking mouthpart. Aphids are small, soft-bodied, pear-shaped insects. The fern aphid is black, but other species are yellow, orange, red, and green. If they've been around for a while, you may also see little, flying adults. Wash them off the plant and try spraying with a soap solution as per the instructions below (just be sure to do a sensitivity test first).

Thrips are tiny insects that also feed on the sap. If present on developing fronds, they too can disfigure or stunt the growth. When feeding, their rasping mouthparts cause an extremely fine mottling, often appearing as silvery white markings, more streaked than dotted. Thrips are hard to detect due to their small size. They can be white, yellow, brown, or black and are slender and elongated, making them look like little lines or dashes. They also jump or fly from spot to spot and can do this before you've even spotted them. The glasshouse thrip is the species known to attack ferns. Many other species prefer to feed on flowers and flower buds, which ferns don't have. Thrips thrive in dry and warm environments, so if the

The center of this plant is infested with fuzzy, white mealybugs, a common pest of indoor ferns.

Scale insects are a common problem on ferns. Wipe them off the plant with a cotton swab dipped in rubbing alcohol.

Mites cause tiny, whitish-yellow stippling on the fronds. Sometimes a fine webbing is also present.

fern is kept in more suitable conditions, it's less likely to suffer a thrips infestation.

Mites are related to spiders and also have eight legs, but they are so tiny—like a very small grain of salt—that many people have a hard time even seeing them. If you knock them off the plant and onto a white sheet of paper, you'll see little, moving specks. Often mite infestations are quite bad before they are even noticed. Mites also feed on plant sap, causing tiny, whitish-yellow stippling on the fronds. Eventually the fronds may turn completely yellow or brown and die. Spider mites spin a fine webbing that you may see wrapped around the fronds. The fern becomes less vigorous and declines. Fortunately, mites are not frequent pests on ferns because they prefer hot, dry conditions. Rinse off any webbing and mites with water, and then try a soap spray as per the instructions on page 87. With a heavy infestation, it is best to dispose of the fern.

Fungus gnats are other insect pests that have become extremely common with potted indoor plants. This is related to the fact that most indoor plants are grown in soilless mixes containing a large amount of organic matter, such as peat moss. Fungus gnats like damp conditions and organic matter. Constantly very moist to wet potting soil benefits these insects, which is another reason not to overwater. You might see adult fungus gnats resting on the fronds, but you'll notice these tiny little black flies when the pot is moved or watered—the disturbance makes the gnats take off. The adults may be annoying, but they are not harmful to your plants. They lay their eggs in the soil, and their larvae feed on the organic matter in the potting soil, and unfortunately, also on the plant's roots. With enough damage to the roots, your fern will not be able to sustain itself. Fronds will begin to yellow or wilt, growth will slow, and the fern will begin to decline. Use yellow sticky cards to trap the flying adults and help you monitor the situation. Consider using biological controls, including Bt (*Bacillus thuringiensis* var. *israelensis*) and beneficial nematodes, to drench the soil and destroy the larvae. Alternatively, allow the top inch (2.5 cm) of the potting mix to dry out between waterings.

Slugs are slimy, land-dwelling mollusks without shells. They can be pests of ferns, particularly *Asplenium* species, but fortunately, slugs are rarely a problem in homes. If the fronds are being eaten, look for the shiny slime trails that are left behind as the slug slides along. They tend to come out at night and hide in moist places, like under pots, during the day. Pick them off and destroy them.

Nematodes are microscopic, wormlike creatures that can feed on roots and foliage. They do not bother

◀ (opposite, left) Adult fungus gnats are easy to trap by hanging yellow sticky cards just above the soil of potted plants.

◀ (opposite, right) Wiping pests off indoor plants, including ferns, is one of the easiest ways to help manage them, though the task is time-consuming.

all ferns, but foliar nematodes can affect the bird's-nest ferns (*Asplenium* spp.) as well as a number of other genera. The "spots" on the fronds are reddish brown or black, and usually angular, taking their shape from the vein pattern. Nematodes can transmit diseases and move in films of water, so keep the fronds dry and prevent splashing of water. Disinfect all tools, pots, soil, and so on before using again, and remove all discolored, infected, and dead leaves. A hot water treatment has been successful on this species. Immerse the plant in hot water (115°F/46°C) for 10 to 15 minutes.

Controlling Fern Pests

It is important to note that ferns are sensitive to chemical pesticides. Always use caution when dealing with any chemical, both for your safety and for your ferns'. It is a good idea to do a small test before a larger application to check the ferns' sensitivity. Always read and follow the directions on the label of any pesticide, even organic ones. The label is the law! Use these products to treat ferns only if the label says it is safe to do so, only use them only for listed pests.

Oil-based pesticides will generally kill ferns. However, the wettable powdered forms are more typically tolerated. When spraying with chemicals, including oils, soaps, or alcohol, avoid spraying soft, young growth if possible. Plants should also not be sprayed if they are wilted, in direct hot sun, or if the temperature is above 90°F (32°C).

Spraying your fern gently with water can dislodge some pests, like mealybugs. This works well on ferns with sturdier fronds, but you need to be more careful on those with delicate fronds. You could add some

mild, liquid dishwashing detergent to the water (1 to 2 teaspoons [5 to 10 ml] per 2 cups [475 ml] of water) to help control some insects. More detergent is more effective against the pest but can also be more damaging to the fern. Remember, ferns are sensitive. Commercially available insecticidal soaps are often too strong for use on ferns and can burn them.

Physical controls are among the easiest and safest to use in the home. Dabbing off pests with cotton swabs dipped in alcohol is laborious but very effective. Use common rubbing alcohol 70 percent, found in many home medicine cabinets, mixed with equal parts water. If you've done a lot of dabbing, rinse off the fern with a little plain water. This not only removes any residue but also washes away any eggs or small critters that remain. Sticky card traps can also be used to catch insects and can help detect an early infestation. Yellow attracts aphids and fungus gnats, while blue attracts thrips. Although these methods won't typically annihilate the problem, if done regularly, they are quick tasks that greatly control damage and prevent the pest from spreading.

Pathogens

Disease pathogens also occasionally affect ferns. There are three main types of pathogens: fungi, bacteria, and viruses.

A *fungus* is a small, usually microscopic organism that feeds on another organism, either living or dead. On fern fronds, spots with halos with lighter edges are typical symptoms of a fungal infection. *Bacteria* are single-celled organisms, and except for cyanobacteria, they cannot make their own food. Discolored, shiny, water-soaked spots on the fronds often indicate a bacterial infection.

Both fungi and bacteria can also rot a fern's root system. Fungal and bacterial infections are usually associated with wet conditions at the root zone or on the fronds. Overwatering and excessive moisture on the fronds create the perfect environment for these pathogens and make it difficult to distinguish disease from cultural issues. Once again, you can see how

Fungal and bacterial diseases can wreak havoc on ferns and other indoor plants, leaving spots and splotches on the leaves, dead fronds, mushy roots, and other symptoms.

When cared for properly, ferns live and grow for many years. Left: *Nephrolepis* 'Fluffy Ruffles'. Right: *Asplenium nidus* 'Crispy Wave'.

important proper culture is. And with fungal and bacterial diseases, an ounce of prevention is certainly worth a pound of cure. Make sure the fern is not planted too deeply, avoid splashing water over the fern, and keep the area clear of dead leaves and other debris. Fortunately, with good culture, these diseases are not a common problem on ferns, especially when they're grown indoors.

Viruses are some of the smallest plant pathogens; they are not even cells. Typical virus symptoms are leaf mottling in a mosaic-like pattern, yellow spots, and distortion. Viruses are not common in ferns, except in the Japanese holly fern, *Cyrtomium falcatum*. When this plant pathogen was studied, it was decided that it was not only a new species of virus, but that it was distinct enough to make a new genus. The pathogen was named the Japanese holly

fern mottle virus (JHFMoV), and it is the only virus known to be transmitted by spores. Viruses are often spread by insects feeding on the sap of an infected plant and then passing it along as they feed on other plants, but viruses also spread through contaminated tools, gloves, and other equipment. Infected ferns are generally not killed, but the yellowing makes them unattractive. There is no cure, and an infected fern should be disposed of.

Pay attention to your ferns, give them the proper care, and show them a little love, and they'll reward you with years of beauty. Remember, a healthy plant is a happy plant!

Rough Maidenhair Fern

BOTANICAL NAME | *Adiantum hispidulum*

If you live in a temperate area where winter temperatures don't reach below 10 to 20°F (-12 to -7°C), rough maidenhair fern grows outdoors. In some warmer parts of the United States, it has started to spread. This is a great indoor fern, usually not more than 12 inches (30.5 cm) tall when potted in a container, where you can easily control its light and moisture needs. Its botanical name comes from its hairy stems and water-repellent foliage.

CULTURE

Grow rough maidenhair fern in bright but not direct sunlight. It needs some light to prosper but not so much as to scorch the leaves. It declines in full shade. Water regularly to keep the soil evenly moist but not waterlogged. A native of rainforests around the world, it likes high humidity but is somewhat tolerant, so a humidity tray is helpful when it's in a very dry environment. Indoors, it prefers temperatures between 60 and 70° F (16 to 21°C). It's also one of the easiest maindenhairs to grow in the home.

PROPAGATION

Propagate by division of clumps or grow from spores.

NOTES

The new leaves emerge reddish pink, giving this fern another common name: rosy maidenhair. Fronds may color in the fall before they go brown and dormant for winter outdoors. The new growth is brighter pink when the plant gets more light. *Adiantum pubescens*, the bronze Venus maidenhair fern is commonly confused with and misidentified as *A. hispidulum*. It is bigger in all respects with an overall similar look, growing 12 to 18 inches (30.5 to 46 cm) tall. Extremely handsome, the new growth is more bronze than red and it is a little more cold tolerant. This species is widely available now.

Southern Maidenhair Fern

BOTANICAL NAME | *Adiantum capillus-veneris*

This fern has the classic maindenhair look that everyone loves with fine, lacy, fan-shaped leaflets on glossy black stems. It grows 6 to 12 inches (15 to 30.5 cm) tall and is winter-hardy outdoors in warmer regions to about 10°F (-12°C).

CULTURE

Southern maidenhair fern chooses its outdoor locations in neutral to alkaline soil, often growing on cool, wet limestone outcroppings in shady to partially shaded areas. Because these conditions can be difficult to replicate in a garden, grow it indoors in a container and provide good drainage and even watering. Avoid overwatering to prevent root rot—maidenhairs do not like wet feet. Southern maidenhair fern grows well indoors, tolerating temperatures down to about 50°F (10°C). They love humidity, so place pots on top of pebbles in a tray, adding water to the top of the pebbles.

PROPAGATION

Propagate by division of clumps or grow from spores.

NOTES

Southern maidenhair fern has a history of food and medicinal use in the many temperate and tropical parts of the world where it grows, including parts of North America, South America, Europe, Asia, and Africa. During its growing season, it can tolerate temporary drought, though it may lose most of its fronds. When moisture returns, new growth sprouts from its base.

Delta Maidenhair Fern

BOTANICAL NAME | *Adiantum raddianum*

This fern, with lovely drooping fronds, can reach 2 feet (61 cm) tall, but in a container it usually doesn't grow more than 12 inches (30.5 cm). It grows well in a terrarium, conservatory, near an indoor water feature, or in any location where high humidity can be maintained to replicate its tropical origins. Formerly called *Adiantum cuneatum*, Delta maidenhair fern is the most common species of maidenhair fern and comes in a variety of cultivars that vary slightly in form, shape, and size, including 'Fragrans', 'Fritz Lüthi', 'Ocean Spray,' and 'Pacific Maid', which is one of the easiest cultivars to grow.

CULTURE

Grow in bright, indirect, or diffused light. Avoid both direct sun, which can fry the leaves, and full shade, which can deplete its vigor. Keep well-drained potting soil consistently moist but not waterlogged. Avoid placing the plant near heat registers or in drafty locations. Add humidity by placing pots on top of pebbles in a tray, adding water to the top of the pebbles. Don't mist maidenhair fronds. Keep the temperature from 55 to 75°F (13 to 24°C).

PROPAGATION

Propagate by division of clumps or grow from spores.

NOTES

Delta maidenhair fern can make a good houseplant and, like many other maidenhairs, often goes through a resting period in the low light of winter. During this time, slightly cooler temperatures, less water, and slightly lower humidity help. Remove any browned foliage immediately to prevent rot. During regular growth, pay attention to browning frond tips, which indicate the fern isn't getting enough humidity.

Brittle Maidenhair Fern

BOTANICAL NAME | *Adiantum tenerum*

With an arching habit cascading downward, the brittle maidenhair fern has fronds that reach up to 3 feet (91 cm) in the wild but only about 12 to 18 inches (30.5 to 46 cm) when grown in a pot. The rhomboidal, bright green leaflets resemble miniature ginkgo leaves. The entire frond spreads out into a fan shape growing on wiry black stems.

CULTURE

This slow-growing fern prefers bright, indirect sunlight or strong artificial light. Keep it evenly moist. Avoid overwatering. It may rest during the winter; clip old fronds as they brown to allow new growth to emerge. Water less during winter dormancy, but never allow the plant to go completely dry. If frond tips go brown, offer more humidity by placing the pot on a humidity tray.

PROPAGATION

Propagate by division of clumps or grow from spores.

NOTES

The best-known cultivar of the brittle maidenhair is 'Farleyense', named for the sugar plantation in Barbados where it was found. It is hardy down to 20°F (-7°C).

Bear Paw Fern

BOTANICAL NAME | *Aglaomorpha coronans*

If you want a big, bold, coarse fern that looks like it came straight out of the age of the dinosaurs, bear paw fern is for you. This leathery, dark green fern grows sturdy, arching foliage that reaches up to 6 feet (183 cm) high in the wild but stays at about 3 feet (91 cm) when kept as a houseplant. Instead of individual leaflets, the edges of the leaves are jaggedly lobed. Like the better-known staghorn fern, bear paw fern is epiphytic or lithophytic—it grows on the surfaces of other plants or on rocks—and can be mounted in a basket or plaque on a tree for an impressive presentation.

CULTURE

Grow bear paw fern in bright, indirect light, planted in a very coarse epiphytic potting mix that allows the soil to drain. This fern likes to stay moist but is tolerant of low humidity and drying out. Don't keep it waterlogged. Let the medium dry out—but not completely—between waterings.

PROPAGATION

Propagate from rhizome cuttings, division if you have a large enough clump, or grow from spores.

NOTES

This fern, a native of tropical Asia, is hardy down to 30°F (-1°C). Its leaves are considered evergreen. It is a sturdy, reliable grower given the right light and temperature. Another common name is crowning bear's claw fern.

East Indian Holly Fern

BOTANICAL NAME | *Arachniodes simplicior*

The East Indian holly fern comes from the woodlands of Japan and China. This elegant fern has long, pointed, sturdy fronds with a handsome leathery texture. The dark green, slightly glossy leaves boast brighter, yellowish green stripes down their centers. In a container indoors, it usually grows 6 to 12 inches (15 to 30.5 cm) tall.

CULTURE

To grow the East Indian holly fern as a houseplant, use standard potting mix. When watering, keep it slightly moist. It will tolerate a little dryness better than being overly wet, which may cause rot. This fern prefers medium to bright light. An eastern exposure is best, but a western exposure is a good alternative, as long as it doesn't get too hot in the afternoon. The thick, leathery fronds of this fern help make it more tolerant of lower humidity levels.

PROPAGATION

Propagate from rhizome cuttings, by division of clumps, or grow from spores.

NOTES

Hardy to 0°F (-18°C), the East Indian holly fern is tolerant of cooler homes. When grown outdoors in colder climates, it isn't reliably evergreen and is very late to awaken in spring. In its native habitat, the East Indian holly fern grows from 1 to 2 feet (30.5 to 61 cm) tall on long, creeping rhizomes that don't make tight clumps. This fern is sometimes listed as *Arachniodes aristata* 'Variegata'.

Japanese Bird's Nest Fern

BOTANICAL NAME | *Asplenium antiquum*

Smaller, but otherwise similar in general appearance to the bird's nest fern (*Asplenium nidus*, see page 97), the Japanese bird's nest fern is attractive and easy to grow as a houseplant as it is a robust grower and tolerates indoor environments well. The main differences between the two are that *A. antiquum* is overall more compact, growing 2 to 3 feet (61 to 91 cm) tall, and has narrower fronds with much shorter stipes. As a houseplant, it probably won't grow more than 1 to 2 feet (30.5 to 61 cm).

CULTURE

Grow Japanese bird's nest fern in well-drained potting soil or on a tree mount. It prefers its rather small root system to be evenly moist; do not overpot or overwater it. Avoid getting water inside the center "nest" to prevent rot. Place it in moderately bright light, such as an east-facing window. Outdoors, it does well with morning light and afternoon shade. If fronds scorch, move it to more shade. Provide extra humidity indoors by placing the plant on a tray with water-covered pebbles. Although it is root-hardy to 40°F (4°C), keep bird's nest fern in indoor temperatures between 60° to 70°F (15.5° to 21°C), no colder than 55°F (13°C). I find this makes an excellent houseplant.

PROPAGATION

Grow from spores. It cannot be divided.

NOTES

There are a number of Japanese bird's nest cultivars, many of them named for people, including 'Leslie' with heavily-forking frond tips, 'Crissie' with irregularly forking frond tips, and 'Osaka' with very wavy frond edges.

Mother Fern

BOTANICAL NAME | *Asplenium bulbiferum*

This plant may be the ideal Mother's Day gift. The mother fern, a native of New Zealand, Australia, Malaysia, and India, also known as a hen and chick fern, grows tiny vegetative growths—miniature ferns—called bulbils on the upper sides of its evergreen fronds. As the bulbils develop into little plants, they drop off the mother fern and grow as clones. The plant, hardy to about 20°F (-7°C) and grows up to 2 feet (61 cm) tall but is usually smaller in pots. It has lacy, identical fronds.

CULTURE

Grow mother fern in a room with moderate light in moist, high-quality potting soil. Good humidity is ideal. Remove old fronds for a tidier appearance. As houseplants, mother ferns do well with normal interior temperatures and tolerate lower light levels.

PROPAGATION

Grow from bulbils or spores.

NOTES

Many—if not most—of the ferns sold as mother ferns have been shown through DNA testing to instead be hybrids, *Asplenium × lucrosum*, a cross between *Asplenium bulbiferum* and *Asplenium dimorphum*. This hybrid is sterile, so it can't produce spores, but it willingly creates bulbils. If your "mother fern" displays two different types of fronds (called dimorphic fronds), you have the hybrid, not the true mother fern. The hybrid, probably brought together by an 1800s plant explorer from plants collected in Australia and New Zealand, may have better vigor than *A. bulbiferum* and is just as easily propagated.

Bird's Nest Fern (or Nest Fern)

BOTANICAL NAME | *Asplenium nidus*

Use your imagination to see the nest: a cluster of unfurled fronds in the center of the vase-shaped plant. In the wild, it's found in trees or on the ground, with fronds up to 5 feet (152 cm) in a clump 8 feet (244 cm) across. As a houseplant, it reaches 2 to 3 feet (61 to 91 cm) tall and wide. Each bright green evergreen frond has a simple spearhead shape with a dark brown rib.

CULTURE

Grow bird's nest fern in well-drained potting soil or on a tree mount. It prefers its small roots to be evenly moist but never waterlogged. Avoid getting water inside the center of the "nest" to prevent rot. Place it in moderately bright light such as an east-facing window. Outdoors, it does well with morning light and afternoon shade. Provide extra humidity indoors by placing the plant on a humidity tray. Although it is root-hardy to 40°F (4°C), keep bird's nest fern in indoor temperatures between 60° to 70°F (16° to 21°C) and no colder than 55°F (13°C).

PROPAGATION

Grow from spores. It cannot be divided.

NOTES

'Crispy Wave' is a variant with very ruffled fronds resembling lasagna. Careful observation reveals that many plants sold in the United States as *Asplenium nidus* are actually *Asplenium australasicum*. However, the differences—longer spore clusters (sori) and differently shaped ribs on *A. australasicum*—won't matter to most people. Both are bird's nest ferns and take similar culture.

Japanese Holly Fern

BOTANICAL NAME | *Cyrtomium falcatum*

This native of eastern Asia, like other ferns that include the word "holly" as part of their common name, grows glossy green leaflets that show a striking similarity to those of the holly shrub. Popular as an easy-to-grow houseplant, it is also grown in the ground in areas where the temperature doesn't reach below 0°F (-18°C).

INDOOR FERN PROFILES

CULTURE

Japanese holly fern can tolerate drier conditions than many other ferns and doesn't need as much humidity. Indoors, it prefers to grow in slightly moist, well-drained soil in bright, indirect light. Avoid allowing the soil to dry out completely or letting the pot sit in water. Keep the indoor temperature between 60° and 80°F (16° and 27°C). In the ground, grow it in partial to full shade or in a location that may get morning sun but is protected from burning sunshine later in the day.

PROPAGATION

Propagate by division of clumps or grow from spores.

NOTES

The 1- to 2-foot-long (30.5 to 61 cm) evergreen fronds tend to sprawl instead of standing upright. Its 3- to 4-inch-long (7.6 to 10 cm) leaflets are leathery rather than delicate. Snip off aging fronds when they begin to decline to allow new foliage to emerge. Cultivars include 'Cristatum', with crested frond tips, and 'Rochfordianum', with deeply cut margins. See Troubleshooting Guide discussion of viruses on page 88.

Squirrel's Foot Fern

BOTANICAL NAME | *Davallia mariesii* var. *stenolepis*

You may want to reach out and pet the soft, furry gray rhizomes on this sweet fern. At first you won't notice them, due to the attractive lacy, triangular fronds that grow 8 to 12 inches (20 to 30.5 cm) tall. In the wild, these ferns are epiphytic, growing on trees and other plants. As houseplants, squirrel's foot ferns are great for hanging baskets, where the attractive rhizomes may creep over the edge of the pot to easily be seen, touched, and admired.

CULTURE

Grow squirrel's foot fern indoors in bright indirect light. An east-facing window location works well. Grow in well-drained, moist but not waterlogged, potting mix. During winter dormancy, reduce watering to keep soil on the drier side. This fern tolerates lower levels of humidity than some others.

PROPAGATION

Propagate by rhizome cuttings or grow from spores.

NOTES

The fronds of the squirrel's foot fern are deciduous. Expect a period of dormancy during the winter, even indoors, with new growth reappearing in spring. Feel free to snip off old, dying fronds to open space for the emerging foliage. A native of eastern Asia and Japan, squirrel's foot fern is hardy to about 30°F (-1°C).

White Paw Fern (or White Rabbit's Foot Fern)

BOTANICAL NAME | *Davallia tyermanii (syn. Humata tyermanii)*

They may not be warm, but all the *Davallia* ferns have a fuzzy side, at least under the leaves. The furry rhizomes of white paw fern, as the name indicates, are white and resemble slender white paws. *Davallia* ferns are epiphytic—they grow on other plants in the wild, especially trees. The rhizomes act somewhat like orchid roots, so while some parts of the rhizomes stay underground, others live above the soil, where they can draw moisture and nutrients from the air. Consider putting white paw fern in a hanging basket at eye level, where the unusual and attractive rhizomes can be seen, admired, and perhaps gently touched.

CULTURE

Grow white paw fern indoors in bright indirect light. Position it in an east-facing window and use a well-drained potting mix. Keep the plant moist but not waterlogged. Reduce watering to keep soil on the drier side during this fern's period of winter dormancy. White paw fern tolerates lower levels of humidity than some others.

PROPAGATION

Propagate from rhizome cuttings or grow from spores.

NOTES

Triangular dark green leaves top this 1- to 2-foot (30.5 to 61 cm) fern, which can tolerate low humidity. It is hardy to 30°F (-1°C). Fun fact: The rhizomes can be trained to grow in a specific direction.

Mahogany Fern (or Tree Maidenhair Fern)

BOTANICAL NAME | *Didymochlaena truncatula*

The young fronds on this handsome vase-shaped fern start out a mahogany color, become more bronze, then eventually transform into their mature color of dark green on stalks of attractive reddish brown. The plant grows 2 to 3 feet (61 to 91 cm) tall and wide but will stay smaller in a container. The leaflets somewhat resemble those of maidenhair ferns.

CULTURE

Mahogany fern is an exception to the rule that ferns love shade; it prefers higher light intensity than most. Avoid the burning rays of direct sun, however. Soft morning light and bright afternoon shade provide an ideal situation. A native of the tropics, mahogany fern also loves and needs high humidity. Most homes aren't humid enough to suit this fern, which makes a humidity tray essential. Plant in well-drained, moist but not waterlogged soil.

PROPAGATION

Grow from spores. If it makes additional side crowns, they can be separated (divided).

NOTES

Although the mahogany fern survives temperatures as cold as 20°F (-7°C), it grows best in temperatures at least 50 to 60°F (10 to 16°C) or warmer. Snip off dead or dying foliage and watch for new growth.

Basket Fern

BOTANICAL NAME | *Drynaria rigidula*

Although there is an entire genus of ferns collectively known as "basket ferns," *Drynaria rigidula* is the only one called by the simple common name of basket fern. It's easy to identify from its two types of fronds. The 2- to 4-foot (61 to 122 cm) fertile green foliage fronds that bear the spores are surrounded by 12-inch (30.5 cm), sterile, rust-colored fronds that form the "basket." In the wild, they can even be mistaken for large bird's nests. The durable basket fronds live for several years and serve a valuable purpose, trapping nutrients in their sturdy stems, such as plant material that breaks down into humus to feed the plant.

CULTURE

Basket ferns grow in the wild on trees or rocks, so they make good hanging plants or can be grown in coarse, well-drained potting soil. Avoid waterlogged soils—this fern is fine if the potting medium goes almost dry before the next watering. Place in filtered light. A tropical native, basket fern is root-hardy to about 30°F (-1°C) but thrives in temperatures of 70 to 80°F (21 to 27°C).

PROPAGATION

Propagate from rhizome cuttings or grow spores.

NOTES

A rare but desirable cultivar of *Drynaria rigidula* called 'Whitei', hailing from the Glass House Mountains of Australia, grows with a more serrated leaf than the species. Basket ferns are sometimes called oak leaf ferns because individual leaflets on fertile fronds bear a resemblance to certain types of oaks.

Heart Fern

BOTANICAL NAME | *Hemionitis arifolia*

It's so easy to fall in love with these little cuties. Heart ferns grow less than 1 foot (30.5 cm) tall and wide. Their leathery, deep green, heart-shaped, 4-inch (10 cm) fronds stand on wiry dark stems. At first glance, you wouldn't even know this plant is a fern.

CULTURE

Grow heart fern in bright, indirect light, avoiding direct sunlight. A north-facing window indoors is ideal. In the wild, this fern grows on trees, but it can also grow in a container, in evenly moist, well-drained soil. Avoid letting the soil go completely dry, as this damages the fronds. On the other hand, don't let this fern rot in waterlogged soil. It likes high humidity and is well suited for growing in a terrarium. To raise the humidity under the fern, place it on a humidity tray.

PROPAGATION

Propagate by spores and the babies that may develop at the bases of the leaf blades.

NOTES

A tropical Asian native, heart fern is hardy to 30°F (-1°C) but prefers to grow in warmer temperatures that are typical of most homes, between 60 and 75°F (16 to 24°C). Heart ferns are readily available from mail-order sources.

Fishtail Fern

BOTANICAL NAME | *Microsorum punctatum (syn. M. polycarpon, Polypodium punctatum)*

The fishtail fern enjoys several other common names, including terrestrial or dwarf elkhorn fern, crested fern, fishtail strap fern, and climbing bird's nest fern. All these names partly describe the unusual form of this evergreen fern's fronds. The 2-foot-long (61 cm), single-blade fronds fork repeatedly, ending in a branched crest that resembles a handsome light green fish tail.

CULTURE

Fast-growing fishtail ferns are epiphytes, meaning they grow on other plants such as trees, but they can also be grown in rich, well-drained soil. Keep the soil moist but not waterlogged. A native of tropical regions, the fishtail fern prefers a warm, humid environment. Provide extra humidity indoors. Keep a sharp eye out for mealybugs and scale insects, which are drawn to this plant and can quickly suck the life out of it.

PROPAGATION

Propagate from rhizome cuttings or grow from spores.

NOTES

Fishtail ferns are hardy to 30°F (-1°C) but prefers to grow in much warmer conditions, from 60 to 80°F (16 to 27°C).

Tuber Sword Fern

BOTANICAL NAME | *Nephrolepis cordifolia*

There's good news and bad news about the tuber sword fern. The good news is that this is a tough, easy-to-grow fern. The bad news is that it's so tough and easy to grow that it's invasive in many temperate and tropical parts of the world, including southern Florida. Its aggressive growth via thousands of wind-borne spores—as well as underground tubers and stolons—creates dense stands of ferns that crowd out native species. If you want to grow this plant, grow it indoors where its spreading habit is contained.

CULTURE

Tuber sword fern grows in partial to full shade but tolerates sun if given enough water. It easily grows in containers. The evergreen leaves last for several seasons. Clip off fronds as they die to improve the overall appearance. Tubor sword ferns tolerate occasional drought.

PROPAGATION

Propagate by division of clumps, tubers, spores, or new plants produced on stolons.

NOTES

Tubor sword fern, a wood fern that grows fronds 2 to 3 feet (61 to 91 cm) long, has many common names, including fishbone fern, tuberous sword fern, tuber ladder fern, ladder fern, erect sword fern, narrow sword fern, and herringbone fern. Its many synonyms include: *Aspidium tuberosum*, *Nephrolepis tuberosa*, and *Polypodium cordifolium*. Tuber sword fern produces tubers, which is one of the main differences between it and its relative the Boston fern (*Nephrolepis exaltata*).

Rita's Gold Boston Fern

BOTANICAL NAME | *Nephrolepis exaltata* 'Rita's Gold'

If the ubiquitous Boston fern leaves you longing for something that's similar, but with a little more flash, the creamy yellow to chartreuse leaves of Rita's Gold Boston fern are for you. Similar but slightly different iterations fall under the names *Bostoniensis aurea*, *Nephrolepis exaltata aurea*, and *Nephrolepis exaltata* 'Aurea' or cultivars such as 'Golden Boston'. All Boston ferns look beautiful in hanging baskets, where their arching foliage creates a highly textured sphere.

CULTURE

Grow Rita's Gold Boston fern in partial to full shade in rich, well-drained soil kept constantly moist but not waterlogged. The golden coloration is best in bright, indirect light. Avoid direct sun, which burns the leaves. Water sparingly in the winter during the fern's normal dormant period. It is hardy to 20°F (-4°C) but prefers to grow in warmer temperatures with good humidity. Optimal temperature is 65°F (18°C) at night and below 95°F (35°C) during the day.

PROPAGATION

Propagate by division of clumps, spores, or new plants produced on stolons.

NOTES

At 18 to 24 inches (46 to 61 cm) tall and wide, Rita's Gold Boston fern is slightly more compact than the regular Boston fern. It is named in honor of Rita Randolph, plantswoman and owner of Randolph's Greenhouses in Tennessee. Grow it as a houseplant or as a seasonal accent plant outside after any danger of frost is past. It adds a punch of color to shady areas.

Macho Fern, Broad Sword Fern

BOTANICAL NAME | *Nephrolepis falcata*

Macho fern can easily be seen from a distance, with handsome green fronds 4 to 6 feet (1.2 to 1.8 m) long.

CULTURE

This large, fast-growing fern is a tropical native. It's hardy to about 20°F (-7°C) but prefers to grow in much warmer conditions. Grow indoors in well-drained soil that is moist but never waterlogged. Add humidity indoors by using a humidity tray. The macho fern prefers bright, filtered sunlight for optimal growth. It can tolerate some direct sun with additional moisture but may not have the best color. In lower light levels, it will grow but not flourish. Trim off any dead or dying fronds.

PROPAGATION

Propagate by division of clumps, spores, or new plants produced on stolons.

NOTES

Like many of its *Nephrolepis* relatives, the macho fern can be a bit of a beast, as its name implies. In Hawaii and southern Florida, it has escaped cultivation and become invasive. Grow it outdoors only in regions where colder conditions will prevent it from spreading and crowding out native vegetation. Macho fern is often misidentified in the trade as *N. biserrata*. *Nephrolepis falcata* 'Furcans', the Fishtail sword fern, which has shorter fronds with forked tips. Zooming in, you can see how Mother Nature took scissors to the sides and ends of each of the leaflets (pinnae) on each frond, dividing the edges and tips into a lively assortment of miniature fishtail shapes.

Sickle Fern

BOTANICAL NAME | *Pellaea falcata*

The sickle fern is relatively small, at 12 to 18 inches (30.5 to 46 cm), with attractive, glossy dark green leathery fronds. Don't expect all the oblong leaflets to look much like sickles, although it's possible a few will curve around in that distinctive shape. New and emerging leaflets are likely to more resemble a heart shape than a sickle. You may find several different shapes on fronds, depending on the age of the frond.

CULTURE

Grow sickle fern in well-drained soil, kept moist but not waterlogged. It needs bright, indirect light indoors.

PROPAGATION

Propagate by division of clumps or grow from spores.

NOTES

This tropical evergreen fern, native to southern Asia, is hardy to 30°F (-1°C) but prefers to grow in much warmer conditions. Sickle fern is touted as a tough fern for ferneries and terrariums. It makes a great container plant due to its relatively compact size. Remove fronds as they decline to make way for new growth.

Button Fern

BOTANICAL NAME | *Pellaea rotundifolia*

This tidy little fern is as cute as a button and needs almost the same amount of care. In other words, button fern is easy to grow, especially as a houseplant. As you might guess from its botanical name, the leaflets are almost round. Growing just 12 to 18 inches (30.5 to 46 cm) tall with leathery, evergreen foliage, this is a good fern for anyone who tends to forget to water.

CULTURE

Grow button ferns in well-drained soil. They don't need as much moisture as some ferns to perform well. Keep the soil on the dry side, but don't let it go completely dry for too long. Yellow, wilted fronds indicate overwatering. It also has less need for humidity, but during winter, indoor conditions may be too dry. Consider placing it in a bathroom or kitchen, where it may get enough humidity. Grow it in bright to medium indirect light.

PROPAGATION

Propagate by division of clumps or grow from spores.

NOTES

Button fern, a native of New Zealand, Australia, and other nearby islands, is cold-hardy to about 25°F (-4°C) but prefers warmer growing conditions, usually 60 to 75°F (16 to 24°C).

Green Cliff Brake

BOTANICAL NAME | *Pellaea viridis* (syn. *Cheilanthes viridis*)

Like its other *Pellaea* fern relatives, the green cliff brake is tough and easy to grow. One of its biggest advantages is that it takes more sun than many other ferns. Cliff brake ferns grow on or among rocks, especially limestone, in various parts of the world. The green fronds with oval leaflets grow 12 to 24 inches (30.5 to 61 cm) long. The plant is hardy to about 25°F (-4°C) but prefers to grow in much warmer conditions.

CULTURE

To grow green cliff brake as a houseplant, plant in well-drained soil. It doesn't require as much moisture as some ferns, so keep the soil lightly watered without going completely dry or completely waterlogged. Yellow, wilted fronds indicate overwatering. Place it in bright, indirect light indoors. Morning light is the perfect indoor situation for green cliff brake fern.

PROPAGATION

Propagate by division of clumps or grow from spores.

NOTES

Green cliff brake fern has become invasive in some warmer parts of the world, so if you live in a tropical area, consider growing it only indoors. It grows well in shaded rock gardens. The botanical label *viridis* refers to its bright green color.

Blue Star Fern

BOTANICAL NAME | *Phlebodium aureum* (syn. *Polypodium aureum*)

Some ferns, like *Phlebodium aurem*, just can't settle on one common name. Here are just a few others: cabbage palm fern, golden serpent fern, gold-foot fern, hare's foot fern, bear's foot fern, and golden polypody fern. Attractive bluish grayish green, deeply lobed fronds covered with golden hairlike scales reach 2 to 3 feet (61 to 91 cm). In the tropics and subtropical areas where it grows wild, blue star fern is epiphytic, growing with its rhizomes firmly attached to trees. The fronds erupt in irregular but delightful "higgledy-piggledy" patterns from the crown.

INDOOR FERN PROFILES

CULTURE

Blue star fern grows in more light and tolerates drier conditions than some ferns, making it a desirable houseplant. Outdoors, it can grow in full sun if it has enough moisture but grows best in partial or dappled shade. Indoors, provide bright indirect light. Grow it in a well-draining potting mix. Many orchid mixes are too porous to provide enough water for this fern, but regular potting soil may be too dense.

PROPAGATION

Propagate from rhizome cuttings, division if you have a large enough clump, or grow from spores.

NOTES

Phlebodium aureum is part of a small, recently discovered genus that split off from the *Polypodium* genus. Most are native to North and South America. It is hardy to 20°F (-7°C) but grows best in much warmer conditions. Cultivars include 'Mandaianum'.

Blue Rabbit's Foot Fern

BOTANICAL NAME | *Phlebodium pseudoaureum* (syn. *P areolatum*, *Polypodium areolatum*)

Blue rabbit's foot fern creeps around on fuzzy reddish orange to brown rhizomes, flashing silvery, bluish gray, deeply lobed fronds that grow 12 to 20 inches (30.5 to 51 cm) tall. The fronds don't all match, and each seems to have its own distinct personality and form. It is closely related to blue star fern, *Phlebodium aureum*. In fact, blue rabbit's foot fern is often sold as *P. aureum*, although they are two distinct species. It is hardy to 10°F (-12°C) but prefers to grow in warmer temperatures.

CULTURE

Blue rabbit's foot fern grows in more light and tolerates drier conditions than some ferns, making it a desirable houseplant. Provide bright, indirect light, and grow this fern in a well-draining potting mix. It will reward you with lovely bluish gray growth.

PROPAGATION

Propagate from rhizome cuttings, division if you have a large enough clump, or grow from spores.

NOTES

Blue rabbit's foot fern goes by other nicknames, including Virginia blue fern. Synonyms include *Polypodium areolatum*, *Polypodium pseudo-aureum* 'Virginia Blue', and *Polypodium pseudoaureum*. The botanical confusion comes because it is part of a small, recently discovered genus that split off from the *Polypodium* genus.

Staghorn Fern

BOTANICAL NAME | *Platycerium bifurcatum*

This fascinating, robust fern grows with two kinds and shapes of fronds, most notably its fertile fronds. These are the irregularly lobed grayish green to bluish green "antlers" up to 3 feet (914 cm) wide that turn cinnamon as they age. Sterile fronds are the rounded, overlapping shieldlike structures at the bases that turn tan or cinnamon. Besides producing spores and offsets (pups), the fertile fronds collect organic materials that feed the fern.

CULTURE

In Southeast Asia where it is native, staghorn fern (also called elkhorn fern) is an evergreen epiphyte that grows on trees. As a result, it needs good air circulation, bright but indirect light, warmth, humidity, and moisture that's absorbed through fronds and rhizomes. When watering, soak the basal fronds as well as the mounting or potting medium. Allow everything to dry between waterings. Both overwatering and letting roots dry out too much can kill staghorn ferns. They look impressive mounted vertically on a wood slab or wire basket but can grow in a well-drained potting medium. Although it is hardy to 20°F (-7°C), wait until temperatures reach at least 50°F (10°C) before moving the plant to a shady spot outdoors for the summer.

PROPAGATION

Propagate by offset division or grow from pores.

NOTES

The large fertile fronds are covered with grayish white furry scales that resemble dust. Don't wipe them off—they are scales that slow moisture loss. Staghorn fern is invasive outdoors in some areas, including Florida and Hawaii.

Caterpillar Fern

BOTANICAL NAME | *Polypodium formosanum*

Although the common name of caterpillar fern isn't terribly appealing, it well describes this fern's odd bluish greenish white rhizomes, which are about the thickness of a large caterpillar, or grub ("grub fern" is another of its other common names). Although the most interesting element of this fern is its rhizomes, the fronds are attractive in a soft green to bluish green. It grows to about 12 to 24 inches (30.5 to 61 cm).

CULTURE

Grow caterpillar fern as an epiphyte mounted on wood, as a lithophyte mounted on rocks, or as a terrestrial grown in a pot. It thrives in partial to full shade in moist, well-drained soil. Water it frequently but allow the medium to partially dry out before watering again. Avoid overwatering or waterlogging the soil. Thanks to its tropical origins in Asia, it also likes high humidity. The caterpillar fern is hardy to about 30°F (-1°C) but grows best in warmer conditions.

PROPAGATION

Propagate from rhizome cuttings, division if you have a large enough clump, or grow from spores.

NOTES

After 1982 when the movie *E.T. the Extra-Terrestrial* was released, this fern and a related cultivar with more bifurcated frond tips, *Polypodium formosanum* 'Cristatum', were marketed as E.T. ferns, relating the rhizomes to the long, thin fingers of the famous movie character.

Korean Rock Fern

BOTANICAL NAME *Polystichum tsus-simense*

With its shiny, dark green fronds and serrated leaflets highlighted with delicate, dark veins, Korean rock fern is a charmer. Growing just 12 to 18 inches (30.5 to 46 cm) tall, it is a reliable houseplant. The fronds grow on dark stems, and the new leaves bear a purple cast until they age to green.

CULTURE

Grow Korean rock fern in moderate light in moist, well-drained soil. Although it can take lower light levels, it needs moderate light to perform best. Avoid overwatering to prevent rot, but be sure the container receives ample water, especially during the summer months. Korean rock fern is hardy to about 0°F (-18°C) and likes temperatures to be warm but not hot. Fronds are evergreen, so you may either clip off dead or dying fronds as they occur or snip the oldest ones before new fronds emerge in early spring.

PROPAGATION

Propagate by division of clumps or grow from spores.

NOTES

Korean rock fern is offered as a house gift in some Asian cultures. The fronds are also used in the cut flower trade, where they often outlast the flowers they are paired with.

Whisk Fern

BOTANICAL NAME | *Psilotum nudum*

Whisk fern was once thought to be a fern ally, but thanks to new evidence, it's now classified as a true fern, though it is the only living vascular plant that has neither leaves nor roots. In botanical Latin, its name means "bare naked," which is certainly appropriate. Whisk ferns have rhizomes covered in hairlike rhizoids, rather than roots. This curious fern predates the dinosaurs and has evolved a special relationship between its rhizomes and a microscopic fungus to provide nutrients. The 6- to 18-inch (15 to 46 cm) plants grow in thick clumps with stiff, upright, green stems that periodically branch into Y-shapes and end with small spherical spore enclosures. People once tied the stems together to serve as small brooms or whisks, giving it the common name.

CULTURE

Whisk fern is native to tropical locations around the world and grows both in trees and on the ground. It is hardy to about 10°F (-12°C) but prefers warmer temperatures for growth. At one time, there were many named cultivars of this plant, but it is now difficult to find in the nursery trade, though in greenhouses and conservatories where it's grown, it sometimes becomes weedy. Whisk ferns prefer moderate light and humidity.

PROPAGATION

Propagate by division of clumps.

NOTES

In Hawaii, this plant is called moa—which means chicken—because the slender stems resemble chicken feet. The spores were used like talcum powder, and children played games with the stems. It is still used in making traditional Hawaiian leis.

Cretan Brake Fern

BOTANICAL NAME | *Pteris cretica*

Yes, you should brake for brake ferns! The words brake and braken, from Middle English, mean a fern or thicket of ferns. The Cretan brake fern, a slow-growing evergreen fern, is a good garden or container size, at 18 to 24 inches (45.7 to 61 cm) tall and wide. Slender, flat green leaflets only about a half inch (13 mm) wide but up to several inches (8 or more cm) long sit along the fronds.

CULTURE

Cretan brake fern is hardy to 20°F (-7°C) and grows best in a warm, humid location. Grow it in bright, indirect light in a sharply drained potting mix. Keep humidity high by placing the pot on a humidity tray. The soil should be kept moist but not waterlogged.

Reduce the amount of water in fall and winter to let the plant go slightly dormant. This fern is evergreen, so clip off dying or dead fronds as needed to allow new growth.

PROPAGATION

Propagate by division of clumps or grow from spores.

NOTES

Cretan brake fern, sometimes called table fern, can be found in attractive forms. The variegated cultivar, *P. cretica* 'Mayii' (also spelled 'Mayi') features heavily forked tips on light green foliage with a narrow cream stripe down the center. Also look for 'Childsii', 'Distinction' and 'Wamsettii'.

Silver Lace Fern

BOTANICAL NAME | *Pteris ensiformis*

Look no further than the common name of silver lace fern to understand something of this fern's appealing looks. Delicate-looking lobed fronds, each touched down the center and along the veins with cream or silver, grow 18 to 24 inches (46 to 61 cm) tall. Some of the oldest and tallest fronds may show a slightly different leaf pattern at the tips. This fern, native to Asia, survives temperatures to about 10°F (-12°C).

CULTURE

Grow silver lace fern in a warm, humid location in bright indirect light to shade. Plant in a sharply drained potting mix. Keep the soil moist but not waterlogged. Reduce the amount of water in fall and winter to let the plant go slightly dormant. Because this fern is evergreen, you'll need to trim off dying or dead fronds to make room for new growth.

PROPAGATION

Propagate by division of clumps or grow from spores.

NOTES

The silver lace fern is also known as sword brake fern. One of the most widely available cultivars of the silver lace fern—and one of the most beautiful—is 'Evergemiensis'. Also look for 'Arguta' and 'Victoriae'.

Spider Brake Fern

BOTANICAL NAME | *Pteris multifida*

The spider brake fern's name seems obvious when you see the fern. Each leaflet is so slender—less than ½ inch (13 mm)—and pointed that it almost seems as if green, long-legged spiders are spilling over the edges of a pot filled with this fern. A common outdoor sight in temperate or tropical areas, it tends to find its way to disturbed soil and cracks in rocks and rock walls.

CULTURE

Grow spider fern in moderate to low light in moist, well-drained soil. Do not allow the soil to become waterlogged but be sure to irrigate this fern regularly. Reduce the amount of water in fall and winter to let the plant go slightly dormant. This evergreen fern needs an occasional trimming when older fronds turn yellow or brown. It is hardy at least to 10°F (-12°C), possibly colder.

PROPAGATION

Propagate by division of clumps or grow from spores.

NOTES

In the United States, this fern is also known as Huguenot fern because it was collected from a Huguenot cemetery in Charleston, South Carolina in 1868, so it was—falsely, as it turned out—believed to have been introduced by the Huguenots. In warm areas of the Southern United States, it has become invasive. The cultivar 'Corymbifera' has crested leaflet tips.

Ribbon Fern

BOTANICAL NAME | *Pteris nipponica* (syn. *Pteris cretica* var. *albolineata*)

Ribbon fern, also known as Japanese silver lace fern, is a real stunner. Each slender leaflet looks as if an artist took a brush and painted a white or cream stripe down the center it, carefully leaving just enough of a green edge to be interesting. The edges of the leaflets are often lightly ruffled. Fronds reach 1 to 2 feet (30.5 to 61 cm) tall.

CULTURE

Cream-lined Japanese brake fern— another name for ribbon fern—is hardy to about 20°F (-7°C) and grows best in a warm, humid location, if grown indoors. To grow it indoors, choose locations with bright, indirect light or moderate light, and plant it in a sharply drained potting mix. The soil should remain moist but never waterlogged. Reduce the amount of water in fall and winter to let the plant go slightly dormant. Dying fronds should be removed as necessary.

PROPAGATION

Propagate by division of clumps or grow from spores.

NOTES

Pteris ensiformis is known as the silver lace fern or slender brake fern. Unless you require a specific fern, it probably doesn't matter which one you get, since they all shine beautifully.

Tongue Fern

BOTANICAL NAME | *Pyrrosia lingua*

Leathery, olive green, single-strap fronds with no lobes and velvety, cinnamon-colored undersides resemble 12- to 18-inch (30.5 to 46 cm) pointed tongues. These tropical ferns naturally grow on trees and rocks in the wild but can make striking houseplants. Each frond has gently wavy edges, giving the illusion of movement even when there is none.

CULTURE

In a container, tongue fern requires an extremely porous soil mix. An even better choice is to mount it on a slab of wood (see Chapter 5 for a how-to on fern mounting). You also can use a wire basket with a fiber lining and sharply draining soil mix. Water consistently but allow the soil to dry out lightly between waterings. Avoid waterlogging the soil. High humidity is another key to its success. Indoors, give this plant bright, indirect light. Good air circulation is a plus. It has slight winter hardiness and can take temperatures to at least 10°F (-12°C), probably colder.

PROPAGATION

Propagate by rhizome cuttings, division of clumps, or grow from spores.

NOTES

Tongue ferns, native to Southeast Asia, are evergreen. Clip off fading or dying fronds as they occur.

Leatherleaf Fern

BOTANICAL NAME | *Rumohra adiantiformis*

Even if you've never grown leatherleaf ferns, you've undoubtedly seen them packaged with many floral arrangements, often with a single long-stemmed rose and baby's breath. The triangular fronds, which grow up to 3 feet (91 cm) long, are durable, valuable players in the cut flower trade. Leatherleaf is native in a wide variety of areas around the globe where temperatures stay above 30°F (-1°C).

CULTURE

Indoors, grow leatherleaf fern in bright indirect light. This slow-growing fern can reach 3 feet (91 cm) wide and 1 to 3 feet (30.5 to 91 cm) tall, depending on growing conditions. Plants stay on the smaller side if they are grown in a container or hanging basket.

Although it is somewhat drought-tolerant, it grows best if you keep the soil moist but not waterlogged.

PROPAGATION

Propagate by division of clumps or grow from spores.

NOTES

This is a relatively easy fern to grow, creating a fluffy yet tidy display. The sizes of the fronds can vary widely. Evergreen leaves look fresh for a long time before they decline. Snip off dead fronds as needed to allow new growth to shine. Keep some on hand for your own cut flower arrangements. Some of its other common names include leather fern, leathery shield-fern, iron fern, 7 weeks fern, and climbing shield fern.

Australian Tree Fern

BOTANICAL NAME | *Sphaeropteris cooperi* (syn. *Cyathea cooperi*)

Looking for a fern from Down Under? You can get down under the Australian tree fern, which can grow as tall as 20 to 30 feet (6 to 9 m) with a trunk 1 foot (30.5 cm) wide. As an indoor plant, it won't get anywhere near that tall, but it will display an umbrella-like set of 8-foot-long (2.4 m) fronds that are reminiscent of palm trees. If you do go underneath, wear protection—the trunk, stems, and undersides of the leaves are covered with bristly brown hairs that can cling to and irritate skin.

CULTURE

Australian tree fern is an understory plant that prefers to grow in partial or dappled shade. Indoors, moderate light is best. It will grow in direct sun if it is well watered but won't be its best. Keep the soil moist but not waterlogged and avoid getting the crown wet to avoid disease. It prefers warmth and high humidity.

PROPAGATION

Grow from spores.

NOTES

Outdoors, Australian tree ferns are hardy to 30°F (-1°C), possibly even 20°F (-7°C). Frost kills its evergreen fronds, but this fast-growing plant can send up new growth. Starting from a low, wide clump, it spreads from 1 foot (30.5 cm) to as wide as 6 feet (1.8 m) in its first year before sprouting upward. Prune off old fronds as needed.

| CHAPTER 4 |

Greening Your Environment

FERNS OUTDOORS

FERNS MAKE ELEGANT, LUXURIOUS ADDITIONS to any garden. Their graceful qualities are calming and they provide peace and serenity in the landscape. As a bonus, ferns are among the easiest perennial plants to care for. The cultural information on the basic needs of ferns presented in this chapter—as well as the information you'll find on how to plant and care for ferns—is universal when it comes to growing ferns outdoors, regardless of whether you garden in a warm or cold climate. However, the ferns profiled at the end of this chapter were chosen for their cold hardiness. They are ferns that can be grown outdoors in temperate zones, where winters mean freezing temperatures. Some of these ferns also grow happily in frost-free regions (see individual fern entries for their specific hardiness).

Although most ferns come from the tropics, the temperate zones are far from lacking in fern diversity. For example, there are more than a hundred species native to the northeastern United States, providing ample choices for growing in a temperate zone. This temperate climate zone forms a band that runs not only across the upper part of the United States and neighboring Canada but continues across the upper parts of Europe and Asia as well. This is why so many of our native plants have "sisters" in Europe and Asia. Having evolved in similar climates and growing conditions, these sister species are often equally at home in our gardens, allowing us all to enjoy these ferns. However, using native species (plants indigenous to your region), often produces the best results with the least effort. Many gardeners see using natives as a more sustainable approach that's healthier for the ecosystem.

◄ (opposite, top) Many ferns that are available to home gardeners perform well in shady areas of the landscape. They look beautiful when combined with other shade-loving perennials and shrubs.

◄ (opposite, bottom) Dappled shade is best for growing ferns. Try to select an area where dappled shade is already present for your fern garden.

Keep in mind that there are many ferns gardeners have yet to be introduced to. There are certainly far more ferns than can be described in any one book, some of which haven't yet been cultivated, indoors or out. Because of this, we really don't know exactly what all these different ferns can tolerate or how adaptable they may be. If you are willing to experiment, especially with a plant that you don't know a lot about, don't be reluctant to give it a go. It may take several tries before you're successful, but you might find your fern grows happily where you didn't expect it to. Sharing your experiences teaches others and makes us all better gardeners as a result!

What a Fern Needs

Growing ferns in your garden is relatively easy, provided you meet three basic needs: light, soil, and moisture. Generally, ferns prefer some shade, loose, rich soil, and ample moisture. Let's discuss each of these needs in greater detail to make sure you have the best environment possible for your ferns.

LIGHT

It's all about the real estate when it comes to growing ferns outdoors successfully. That means location, location, location! With only a few exceptions, all ferns prefer some shade. Ferns usually exhibit their best growth with bright, indirect light. They do not like hot midday sun. Think "skyshine," not sunshine. Open wooded areas with high canopy shade from deciduous trees, dappled shade where light flickers through the

TROPICAL CLIMATE GARDENERS

Because most ferns are native to moist, tropical regions, the more tropical your climate, the broader the palette of species you'll have to choose from. If you garden outdoors in a tropical or subtropical climate, be aware that some of the cold-hardy ferns profiled later in this chapter may not grow without sufficient chilling. See the profiles included in chapter 3 to make choices for your garden. The ferns profiled there will likely thrive outside in a tropical or subtropical region like yours. In these areas, you might also be able to grow epiphytic fern species outside, mounted right in your trees.

leaves, areas that receive early morning or very late afternoon sun, open, unobstructed northern exposures (in the Northern Hemisphere), or any areas shaded by a fence, house, or even tall city buildings are all ideal settings for ferns when it comes to available light. The deep shade found under most evergreens or dense shade trees, such as maples and beeches, is too dark for many ferns. Avoid sunny, hot, dry spots.

Although it is possible to alter the amount of sun or shade an area receives, doing so is complicated and can take years to achieve. Trees in wooded areas that are too dense can be pruned and thinned by an arborist to let in more light and air. This may make an immediate change, but it requires continued management. Removing light-obstructing structures is often not an option. And although it's possible to create some shade by putting up structures, such as arbors or lath, this requires time, effort, and money. Trees can certainly be planted to provide shade, but typically they take years to be effective. The point is, you should try to select an area that's already naturally shady for your ferns so you don't have to manipulate the environment too much.

SOIL

The soil is a fern's home. Almost all outdoor ferns prefer rich, organic soils with good drainage. A loose, open soil structure allows for good drainage and keeps the soil well aerated. The organic matter found in soil holds essential water and nutrients and helps to build and maintain good soil structure. Most gardeners aren't lucky enough to start out with such ideal soil. If you can find ferns that tolerate your natural soil conditions, by all means plant them. If not, don't despair.

Fortunately, with a little effort, soil can be improved and amended to suit fern growth. Your soil might be anywhere on the spectrum from dry, light, sandy soil to heavy, wet, clay soil. Whatever type of soil you have, you can make it more to your fern's liking. Soils that are very sandy drain well and are well aerated. These traits are excellent for ferns because ferns need good drainage and good aeration. Sandy soil is generally loose and open. However, it doesn't hold nutrients or water well, and dries out too quickly. Alternatively, if your soil is heavy clay, it holds moisture and nutrients well but often does not drain sufficiently. Clay soil lacks adequate amounts of air and is not open and loose enough for most ferns. Remember, ferns tend to have small, delicate, wiry, shallow root systems and therefore don't usually like heavy soils. And ferns can't tolerate soil compaction. Because of this, it's best to keep ferns away from heavily trafficked areas and trees and shrubs with big, shallow root systems that compete for water and make it difficult for ferns to grow.

What all this means is that, whether you have sandy soil, clay soil, or something in between, the best solution is to add organic matter. Compost, leaf mold, and composted manure are great organic amendments for improving your soil. Organic matter bulks up sandy soil, providing water and improving nutrient retention, while still retaining its light, open structure. In a clay soil, organic matter builds good soil structure, opening pore spaces and improving drainage and aeration. When preparing clay soils for ferns, it is especially good to add some gypsum, which helps to further open the structure and provides calcium, a nutrient that benefits ferns greatly.

Preparing the Soil for Planting

To add organic matter to your soil prior to planting ferns, incorporate it by digging it in to the soil 6 to 8 inches (15 to 20 cm) deep. First, remove any weeds from the area, and then spread 2 inches (5 cm) of organic matter (any combination of the aforementioned will work) over the soil's surface. Using a garden fork, spade, or shovel—depending on how soft or hard your soil is—dig the organic matter into the entire area. Lift the soil up slightly out of the hole and turn it over, dropping the top of the soil (with the organic matter) into the bottom of the opening you've just created. This greatly improves the condition of the soil, and your ferns will be thrilled! If the area has never been amended, consider adding a general-purpose, granular, organic fertilizer to the soil surface before turning in the organic matter.

It is best to prepare the entire planting area instead of just the individual planting holes if you are planning to plant several ferns. Alternatively, you might choose to raise the soil level for any number of reasons. Perhaps you want to do so for design or maintenance purposes, or maybe your soil is very hard and compacted. If possible, try breaking up and loosening the soil surface and then adding 6 to 8 inches (15 to 20 cm) of new topsoil on top, effectively creating a raised bed. If desired, you can contain the bed with a stone edge, wooden planks, or another material. Use a loamy topsoil mixed with organic matter and a sprinkling of organic fertilizer for the best results. If you're working with a reclaimed site and are concerned about the potential for toxic

▲ Amending the soil with organic matter prior to planting your ferns is a good way to ensure they receive good drainage and ample nutrition.

▶ Most ferns, including this Japanese painted fern, prefer a soil pH that's slightly acidic. Test your soil and adjust as necessary to keep your ferns healthy and happy.

compounds or elements in your soil, it is best to take a soil test for confirmation. In such a case, you might choose to replace the soil, or at the very least, build a raised bed filled with imported soil.

Adjusting the Soil pH

Like most other plants, most ferns prefer a slightly acidic soil with a pH range of 6 to 7. If possible, conduct a soil test before doing any work on your soil. Send a sample to a lab or buy a simple test kit online or from your local nursery and check the pH yourself. If the pH needs to be adjusted, address that need as you amend and prepare your soil for planting. Along with organic matter and possible fertilizer, if necessary, apply the appropriate material to correct the pH. If other ferns you have in the area are thriving, most likely your pH is within their desired range. But if your soil test result indicates the soil is too acidic and you need to raise the pH, use dolomitic limestone, ground limestone, or pulverized oyster shells. Conversely, if the test tells you the pH is too alkaline and you need to lower the pH, use ground sulfur or aluminum sulfate. Note that some ferns prefer a slightly alkaline (basic) soil with a pH of 7 to 8, and some prefer more acidic conditions, with a pH range of 4 to 7. Instead of altering the existing pH, another option is to choose varieties that are adapted to your specific conditions.

WATER

Most garden ferns like to be kept evenly moist, and a well-prepared soil maintains proper moisture levels, keeping the ferns healthier and making less work for you. As with any new planting, keeping your ferns properly watered is critical to their establishment.

◀ In general, outdoor ferns need a minimum of 1 inch (2.5 cm) of water per week throughout the growing season. If no rainfall occurs, plan to irrigate your plants as necessary.

When acquiring plants, always use reputable sources. Ferns grown responsibly are healthy and free of diseases and pests. They should be ethically sourced and grown, and not collected from the wild. Never collect plants from public lands or private land without permission from the landowner. Even with permission, act responsibly and check to make sure you are not collecting any species that might be protected, rare, threatened, or endangered.

Water regularly for the first year, after which the ferns should be well established. Once established, fern plantings are generally low maintenance and tolerant of short periods of dryness.

In areas with consistent year-round rainfall, you might never need to water. Other areas that receive ample rain during the spring and fall won't usually need water during those seasons. However, if you garden in such a climate, you may need to water during the hotter, drier summer months. Whatever your location, be mindful of droughts or dry spells and heat waves during the growing season and provide additional water as needed. Some ferns tolerate dryness a little better than most, while other ferns prefer wet conditions. It is always best to match the ferns' needs as closely as possible to your site conditions.

On average, a general irrigation guideline for gardens is 1 inch (2.5 cm) of water per week during the growing season. The water should reach down at least 6 inches (15 cm) into the soil, to make sure the root zone area is sufficiently moistened. Don't assume a passing summer shower will deliver the needed amount of water. Get a rain gauge to measure rainfall in your garden for more accuracy. Soaker hoses and drip irrigation are the best ways to water when there isn't enough rainfall, and they are the most efficient, too. Overhead watering can beat down fern fronds, mar fronds that are delicate, encourage and spread disease, and cause fronds to stay wet for extended periods of time. And overall, overhead irrigation is very wasteful.

Rain barrels offer a sustainable way to collect water to be used when needed. Some ferns, particularly *Adiantum*, *Athyrium*, *Matteuccia*, and *Onoclea* may brown prematurely if they get too dry in the middle of the season. Avoid windy, exposed sites. Few ferns can tolerate wind—it is too desiccating. Fronds dry out, and the more gentle, delicate fronds break as they get whipped about.

TEMPERATURE

Once you have identified, or created, a suitable site to grow your outdoor ferns, the remaining consideration is temperature. Be certain to select plants that will survive in your overall climate. Although cold-hardiness is not the only climate-related factor that can affect or limit plant growth, it is a defining one, and it is a longstanding practice to categorize plants by how much cold they can tolerate. In the United States, use the USDA Hardiness Zone Map to find your growing zone. You can also go online to use the interactive version. These zones are based on how cold it gets, or the minimum temperatures for each zone. In the UK, use the Royal Horticultural Society's hardiness zone map. There are hardiness zone maps for Canada, Australia, Europe, and several other countries and regions as well. Consult these maps to determine the lowest average winter temperatures where you live. This information comes in handy when deciding whether a particular fern will be winter-hardy in your garden. Keep in mind, however, that microclimates exist in many places and affect the ability of plants to grow.

For the fern profiles included at the end of this chapter, I've noted the lowest temperature each different species can tolerate. Use this information to determine if the fern is a good fit for your landscape.

Planting Ferns

There are two primary ways new ferns arrive in your garden: as potted plants and as existing plants that are being moved from elsewhere in your own garden or from the garden of a friend. Let's look at the best planting practices for both.

HOW TO PLANT A POTTED FERN

To plant a containerized fern in the garden, water it thoroughly the day before planting. When ready, put your hand over the top of the pot, spreading your fingers around or between fronds as needed, and tip the pot over, tapping or shaking the plant out. It should come out easily. If it's extremely well-rooted in the pot and it's a cheap plastic pot, cut the pot away if necessary.

Next, look at the rootball. If it is very dense and the roots were circling inside the pot, the rootball should be loosened before putting it into the soil. Massage the rootball with your fingers and hands, loosening the roots so they can spread out into the surrounding soil after planting. If the fern remains rootbound when planted, the roots may stay in their tightly wound position and never grow out into the soil around them.

Never lift a fern by its fronds, Instead, handle it by the rootball. If you have already prepared the bed as discussed previously, simply dig a hole the same depth as the rootball but a little wider and place the fern into the planting hole. Keep the soil line of the rootball even with the surrounding soil. Make sure that the growing tips of the rhizomes are just above the soil line—if they're buried, they may rot. A tiny bit higher is better than deeper.

Next, begin to fill in with soil around the rootball. Fill 4 to 6 inches (10 to 15 cm) of soil at a time, and then firm gently all the way around the rootball with your fingers pointing straight down. Repeat in intervals of 4 to 6 inches (10 to 15 cm) until the hole is backfilled completely. Water the fern in, making

sure water soaks the entire rootball as well as the surrounding soil. If the soil level drops down after watering, add more soil to bring it up to level. Be careful not to overdo it. The idea is to remove air pockets from around the rootball and prevent the soil from settling unevenly, not to compact the soil.

If you have not amended the soil as discussed previously, dig the hole the same depth as the rootball but about three times wider. Set the fern in the hole and follow the directions given above. Add a little organic matter to the backfill soil but mix it thoroughly before you start returning the soil to the hole. Wide digging like this is done to physically loosen the surrounding soil, making it easier for the roots and rhizomes to grow out. Fill and gently firm this area too, keeping it all level.

If you had to do a lot of loosening to the rootball, the fern may suffer from transplant shock. For this reason, it is better to purchase a plant that isn't so rootbound whenever possible. Make sure you give the fern extra attention, and check for watering needs daily if possible. Keep your eye on the fern. You may have to prune off some of the fronds or cut them in half to compensate for the root loss and keep the plant in balance. If it goes into severe shock and wilts completely, try to provide some extra shade while it rebounds over the following weeks. Make a covering or tent out of burlap or a white pillowcase and stakes. This reduces light and air flow, taking stress off the fern.

HOW TO PLANT A TRANSPLANTED FERN OR DIVISION

Upon replanting a fern that has been dug out of the ground, whether it's been divided or not, pay close

◄ When you receive fern divisions from friends, try to keep as much soil on the roots as possible and replant them as quickly as you can.

attention because it will likely need some extra nurturing. When digging out ferns for replanting or division, try to maintain a good rootball. If fern plants or divisions arrive with very little soil on the roots (called bare-root), soak the entire plant in a bucket of water for a few hours before planting. If planting is delayed, wrap the bare-root ferns in wet newspaper or burlap. You can even put the wrapped plants in a plastic bag in the shade to keep them cool and moist and prevent them from drying out for a few days. Plant these ferns as soon as possible, and follow the recommendations on the previous page for planting and special aftercare.

When transplanting a fern plant or fern division with a long, creeping rhizome, you generally want the tip of the rhizome to be just above the soil. For these ferns, there's no need to dig a hole because they are generally quite shallow and very wide. It is best to dig a little trench or trough and place your rhizome in that. Cover lightly with some soil. The rhizome should be at most ½ to 1 inch (1.3 to 2.5 cm) deep, and the tip where the growing point is should be aimed upward and at or slightly below the surface of the soil.

Always be certain to water in the transplanted fern thoroughly once you've finished planting. When watering, try not to water over the top of the fern, wetting all the fronds. Instead, soak the rootball and the surrounding soil after you firm the plant in. This eliminates any air pockets, settles the soil, and moistens the entire area, encouraging the roots to grow out. If necessary, you can gently wash off soil from the fronds.

With planting and watering completed, the next step is mulching. Shredded leaves, leaf mold and compost, and fine bark or wood chips are perfect companions for ferns. Apply a layer 1 to 2 inches (2.5 to 5 cm) deep, covering the soil all around the fern but making sure that the mulch never touches the plant tissue directly.

Spring and early fall are the recommended seasons for fern planting. Depending on your climate, you might prefer one over the other. You can plant ferns in summer if you must but be very careful to make sure they're well watered. It's always best to avoid particularly hot spells.

One thing to keep in mind is that if your fern has a lot of new, soft, tender growth, it is not a good time to disturb it. Wait until the young fronds mature and toughen a little before you dig it up and change its surroundings. New, tender growth is vulnerable and will likely be damaged or lost if disturbed in the delicate developing stage.

Seasonal Outdoor Fern Care

Ferns are low-maintenance perennials and do quite well with only occasional help from us gardeners. Now that you have ferns growing in your garden, let's look at what care is required through the seasons, particularly in temperate regions.

EARLY SPRING FERN CARE

Early spring, just before new growth begins, is the time to finish any cutting back and cleaning up that wasn't done at the end of the previous season. It is important to do this before the new fiddleheads emerge so as not to damage them. Some people may leave on old, brown fronds as a form of mulch, offering some protection to the crown and roots of the fern through winter. Early spring is the time to cut them away and remove the debris. Compost the old fronds or shred them and return them to the garden as mulch.

Evergreen ferns have fronds that usually remain green through winter, even in the snow. Some of these ferns may keep their form and stay more upright, but others eventually lie down, often by midwinter. Either way, it is best for evergreen ferns if you leave the fronds on for the winter. They are photosynthesizing and providing some insulation. By early spring, trim away the old fronds in preparation for new growth. Some may look a little more weathered and tattered, and you won't mind cutting them, while others may look perfectly fresh. But, know that they too will begin to yellow and die as the new growth takes over. If you wait, it becomes very tedious and difficult to cut them away without damaging the new growth.

Once the ferns and the bed have been cleaned of debris, the best thing you can do for your ferns is to put a 1- to 2-inch (2.5 to 5 cm) topdressing of compost or leaf mold. This should be done annually at the beginning of the season, or you can put about 1 inch (2.5 cm) down now and then in midsummer apply another. Don't work, scratch, or cultivate it into the soil. Remember, ferns have delicate, shallow roots, and we don't want to disturb or destroy them. This annual application of organic matter provides all the nutrition ferns need and supplies the soil with the necessary organic components to keep the soil's food web functioning and self-sustaining. This is all you have to do to maintain good soil qualities.

If you feel that you need to put down some fertilizer, early spring is also the time to do it. Ferns are not heavy feeders and are sensitive to some fertilizers, so I recommend using an organic one. Apply a granular, all-purpose, organic fertilizer at half the recommended rate. Organic fertilizers are derived from natural substances, such as kelp and fish, and have very low percentages of nutrients. For these reasons organic fertilizers are less likely to burn your ferns and are better for the environment. They will also not kill the living organisms that are essential to the health of the soil. An all-purpose fertilizer has some of each of the three major nutrients: nitrogen (N), phosphorous (P), and potassium (K), and preferably some minor nutrients as well. The three numbers on the label, representing the percentages of N, P, and K, should not add up to more than 10. If you choose to add supplemental fertilizer, it's better to sprinkle it

◄ Early in the spring, new fiddleheads emerge from your outdoor ferns. They are very fragile, so as you clean up the garden, be careful not to disturb them.

▶ Keep fern beds mulched with shredded leaves or bark chips to stabilize soil moisture levels and limit weeds.

onto the soil first, and then spread the organic matter over it.

After putting down fertilizer (if you choose to do so) and spreading the organic matter, cover it all with a thin, ½-inch (13 mm) layer of mulch, if you'd like. Use shredded leaves or fine bark chips. The organic matter and mulch are incredibly important, especially for ferns. The covering helps to retain moisture and keep the soil temperature from fluctuating, which is very helpful in protecting those shallow roots. It also suppresses weeds and prevents and reduces compaction due to rain or watering, keeping your soil soft and in good condition. Using bark chips or shredded leaves adds more organic matter to the soil as well. Check the mulch again in mid to late fall. Even if you already put down mulch in the spring, it may have decomposed or worn away. If this is the case, refresh it with ½ inch to 1 inch (1.3 to 2.5 cm) in the fall to provide a little protection through the winter.

SEASON-LONG CARE

Throughout the growing season, regular maintenance includes watering as needed, removing weeds, scouting for possible diseases, pests or problems, and grooming your plants as needed. Should any leaves get damaged, break or die, cut them off and clean up the plant to keep it looking its best.

END-OF-SEASON CARE

As fall approaches, especially in temperate climates and anywhere there are deciduous shrubs or trees, you may choose to do some leaf cleanup as the deciduous trees drop their leaves. It's fine to allow a thin layer of leaves to remain on the soil around your ferns as a natural mulch but remove heavy accumulations. Don't, however, leave the crowns of your ferns (the growing centers) buried deep under leaves, or they might stay too wet and rot. Be very careful when using rakes around ferns, as ferns are easily loosened or dislodged and damaged.

Many temperate garden ferns die back sometime during the fall. As they turn yellow, or even brown, if they remain upright, leave them intact to add interest and seasonal color to the garden. When the fronds collapse or fall, pick them up or cut them off. Work by

hand with pruning shears for the best results. Those who like tidy gardens often clean up their ferns in the fall and compost or shred the debris. However, some growers don't mind the look and recommend that you leave those brown fronds in place. As they lie down around the plant, the old fronds offer a bit of winter insulation. In this case, clean them up in early spring, before new growth begins.

▲ At the end of the growing season, most ferns turn yellow or brown. You can cut these fronds off in the fall or early the following spring, before new fiddleheads emerge.

▶ Ferns make beautiful additions to gardens big or small. Their cool, green foliage adds a lush and inviting touch.

Troubleshooting Guide

As far as pests, problems, and diseases go, outdoor garden ferns are relatively trouble-free. Even if there is a problem, the damage is rarely severe. If you have deer in your area, it's extremely rare for them to eat your ferns. I've found that to be the case in many places, even with very large deer populations. Some people complain of problems with rabbits nibbling or even devouring their ferns, but again, even with abundant rabbit populations, I have never experienced or even seen this.

FERN PESTS

Slugs and **snails** are perhaps the most universal complaint among fern gardeners. Slugs seem to have an affinity for some *Asplenium* species, and I have seen this on occasion. Low dishes of beer placed throughout the garden trap them, and diatomaceous earth sprinkled around the ferns work quite well to control these pests. So do midnight raids to pick them off and drown them in soapy water.

Occasionally **aphids** descend upon young, tender fern growth, especially in spring. I've only seen it on rare occasions, and the damage was not even noticeable. Aphids generally don't stay around long, and control is rarely an issue (see more about aphids in the troubleshooting section of Chapter 3 on page 85).

I have read of **leaf roller caterpillars** causing damage, but have no personal experience with them on ferns, though I have seen them on many other plants. Apparently they are not huge fern pests, but when they do take up residence on a fern, their damage is noticeable. They usually attack developing fronds; they gather the little leaflets and bundle everything together, completely disfiguring the frond. There they feed and remain until they emerge as moths. Picking them off by hand is reported to work.

Leaf-hoppers are another pest I have experienced with many other plants, but I am happy to report that I have not experienced them on ferns. They are small, pale green insects that feed on the fern, leaving tiny white dots that mar the appearance of the frond. Leaf-hoppers blend in very easily and are often noticed only when you brush against the plant and they all hop off at once. Leafhoppers generally will not kill the fern, and chemicals are about the only way to control them.

FERN DISEASES

Diseases that attack the foliage or roots (root rot) of ferns are not common and are usually due to poor growing conditions. Keep the fronds dry and provide good air circulation to stop diseases from attacking the fronds. Make sure the soil is well drained and doesn't stay soggy to prevent root rot. Remove any diseased fronds or plants and discard in the trash immediately. And lastly, don't forget the impact of people on the health of your ferns! Ferns cannot tolerate a lot of foot traffic, and invasive recreational activities can be disastrous to these plants.

Maidenhair Fern

BOTANICAL NAME | *Adiantum aleuticum* (Western species) and
Adiantum pedatum (Eastern species)

These two closely related species were formerly considered one species, *A. pedatum*. Although the native range of *A. aleuticum* is west of the Rocky Mountains, and *A. pedatum* is generally in the northeast corner of the United States, the two share most physical traits and cultural needs and are difficult to tell apart. Wiry and strong purple-black stems reaching 1 to 2 feet (30.5 to 61 cm) tall support delicate-looking, bright green fronds that spread out almost like an open human hand, lending this plant another common name, five-finger maidenhair fern.

CULTURE

Maidenhair fern grows in a wide variety of light conditions, from scant to deep shade, and in most soils, from sand and loam to clay. Its unfussy requirements make it a great choice in a shade garden, where it prefers light shade and soil that stays evenly moist but never waterlogged. Avoid placing this fern where hot late afternoon sun could blast and burn its leaves.

PROPAGATION

Propagate by division of clumps or grow from spores.

NOTES

Hardy down to about -35°F (-37°C), maidenhair fern lends an airy, ethereal texture to shade gardens until fall, when it sheds its leaflets to go into winter dormancy. The leaves form about halfway up the stalks, allowing undergrowth to be seen under these frothy skirts. Clumps form slowly, so purchase multiple plants and space them about 2 feet (61 cm) apart if you have a larger area to fill in. They will not grow in the warmest zones. The western species is easier to grow and is the one typically available. The new leaves emerge green and the middlemost pinna, the "finger," is longer than the others and sticks out. The eastern species has fronds that emerge a rosy color before turning green and a more even, rounded outline.

Himalayan Maidenhair Fern

BOTANICAL NAME | *Adiantum venustum*

The pleasing arrangement of teardrop-shaped, soft green leaves on graceful arching black stems vaults the Himalayan maidenhair fern into favorite status for many fern lovers. As you might guess from its name, this fern is native to chilly regions of Asia and flourishes in cool, moist conditions but has much the same look and delicate beauty of the tropical maidenhairs.

CULTURE

This fern is evergreen in the milder parts of its range. Cut back the old fronds to their bases—even if they're still in good shape—before new growth in late winter to early spring to allow the fresh new bronze-pink growth to emerge and shine. Though it will grow in clay or sandy soils, for best results plant Himalayan maidenhair fern in humus-rich soil with excellent drainage. Do not plant the rhizomes too deeply. Keep the soil moist but not waterlogged. It prefers a location with morning sun and afternoon shade, though it will grow in full shade.

PROPAGATION

Propagate by division of clumps or grow from spores.

NOTES

Hardy down to -25 to -30°F (-32 to -34°C), Himalayan maidenhair fern is a 6- to 12-inch (15 to 30.5 cm) charmer that can widen to a patch about 3 feet (91 cm) wide after 5 to 10 years of careful tending and good soil. It struggles in regions with hot, humid summers, even with extra attention and moisture to grow well. The payoff comes from the airy, delightful sprays that add texture to a shade garden. It can also thrive in a container.

Dragontail Fern

BOTANICAL NAME | *Asplenium ebenoides (syn. Asplenosorus × ebenoides)*

Roaring to life but raising its spiky leaves a mere 4 to 12 inches (10 to 30.5 cm) tall, the dragontail fern might become a kid's or dinosaur lover's favorite. Native to the Eastern United States, the dragontail fern is a natural, whimsical hybrid cross between two other species of *Asplenium*. In the wild, this fern grows on or near calcareous rocks, making it an excellent choice for rock gardens.

CULTURE

Grow in partial to full shade. Dragontail fern tolerates most soil types, but does best in moist, well-drained soil. Though it is somewhat slug-resistant, these pests may find it worthy of a nibble.

PROPAGATION

Propagate by division of clumps. This hybrid is sterile and cannot grow from spores, except for one population in the southern US. These fertile plants are being cultivated and are helping to make this plant more widely available. If you have the fertile variation, you will be able to grow it from spores.

NOTES

Though the name dragontail is more evocative of its looks, this fern is also known as Scott's spleenwort, named for R. Robinson Scott, who identified it as a new species in 1861. With its short stature and unusual leaf structure, it works well as an edging plant in a rock garden where it can be easily seen and admired. Or, place it in a container where light and water are easy to control. It also makes a good subject for a terrarium. It multiplies and spreads slowly to a clump 8 to 12 inches (20 to 30.5 cm) wide. It tolerates temperatures down to -25 to -30°F (-32 to -34°C). It's evergreen, but cut back old stems before new growth begins in early spring to keep the clump looking tidy.

Hart's-Tongue Fern

BOTANICAL NAME | *Asplenium scolopendrium* (syn. *Phyllitis scolopendrium*)

This species is native to North America and Europe. The North American plant is *A. scolopendrium* var. *americanum*, and it is very rare and difficult to grow, only growing in soils with lime. It should never be collected! The European plant is *A. scolopendrium* var. *scolopendrium*; it is abundant and easy to grow. All plants in cultivation are the European species. Its common name comes from Europe, where mature red male deer were called harts in medieval times. It's easy to see how it got this name: Long, strap-like fronds unroll, radiating out from a central point and giving the impression of extra-long tongues rising straight up from the earth. Wavy edges on shiny green leaves add an attractive element to a clump.

CULTURE

Grow in partial to full shade in slightly moist soil. To keep the soil moisture even and consistent, mulch around the plants with compost, but be sure the soil drains well or the roots will rot.

This fern prefers alkaline soils. If your soil is acidic, amend it to raise the pH or add some calcium. Hart's-tongue fern does not like regions with hot, humid summers.

PROPAGATION

Propagate by division of clumps or grow from spores.

NOTES

Hart's-tongue fern looks almost tropical, making it easy to remember that it's hardy only down to about 0 to -10°F (-18 to -23°C). The 8- to 16-inch-tall (20 to 41 cm) deep green straps rise almost vertically, adding an interesting punctuation to shade garden plantings. The evergreen leaves may be snipped off when they lose vigor with age. Their unfurling fiddleheads were used as the scroll pattern on the necks of violins. Victorians in England listed more than 400 varieties of hart's tongue fern. Their fronds take on varying forms and are favorites of collectors.

Maidenhair Spleenwort

BOTANICAL NAME | *Asplenium trichomanes*

With a common name like spleenwort, this fern could have a real public relations problem. Luckily, it enjoys and shares some of the lovely, airy qualities of maidenhair fern (*Adiantum*) fronds, as well as dark stems. Despite its diminutive stature, it is one tough character. Maidenhair spleenwort appears in temperate climates on all continents but Antartica, clinging to rocky habitats, which is a clue about how it best likes to grow.

CULTURE

Grow maidenhair spleenwort in almost any kind of moist, well-drained soil in partial to full shade. One of the two subspecies, a diploid shows a preference for slightly acid soils; while the other, a tetraploid, loves lime. It tolerates dry shade once its root system is established. The roots will rot if left in waterlogged soil. Its best-case scenario is to find a crevice where moss can keep its roots covered and moist.

PROPAGATION

Propagate by division of clumps or grow from spores.

NOTES

Tuck this little fern into gaps in rock walls or in rock gardens, where it will make a perfect small statement. Soil splashed on the fronds can stunt their growth, so use moss, rocks, or mulch to prevent this. The fronds on this 4- to 12-inch-tall (10 to 30.5 cm) fern are evergreen—just snip off tired stalks when they are past their prime. Hardy down to about -20°F (-29°C), maidenhair spleenwort is slow growing but easy to tend in a garden. Grow as a companion among bonsai plants or in a terrarium.

Lady Fern

BOTANICAL NAME | *Athyrium filix-femina*

Graceful lady ferns bring frothy elegance to a shade garden. These frilly, light green ferns are so readily adaptable that it's likely you've seen them in wild settings around North America. Their exuberant growth by underground rhizomes can sometimes move out of bounds in a garden, but they are easy to control and share or discard. *A. filix-femina* var. *angustum*, the northern lady fern, is native to North America and is also known as Lady in Red. *A. filix-femina* var. *filix-femina* is the European lady fern. Victorian England had around 300 named varieties in cultivation, and some are still available. You can find European lady fern cultivars with unusual traits such as cresting (*A. filix-femina* 'Cristatum'), crossing (*A. filix-femina* 'Cruciatum'), and feathery (*A. filix-femina* 'Plumosum' group) foliage.

CULTURE

Lady ferns are no exception to the general rule that ferns prefer moist soil in partial to full shade. But they are amenable to many conditions and may tolerate dry soil but will likely brown out or die back. This 1- to 3-foot-tall (30.5 to 91 cm) fern even grows in sun if the soil is kept uniformly moist but not waterlogged.

PROPAGATION

Propagate by division of clumps or grow from spores. Spore-grown offspring will usually not look like the parent. Spores may self-sow in rich, moist soil.

NOTES

The fronds can be somewhat brittle, so protect lady ferns from foot traffic and areas prone to high winds. By the end of the growing season, just before they lay down their fronds and go dormant for the winter, lady ferns may stop looking their best. Feel free to snip off any unsightly parts as the season progresses. Dormant rhizomes survive winters as cold as -20 to -30°F (-29 to -34°C).

Japanese Painted Fern

BOTANICAL NAME | *Athyrium niponicum* 'Pictum'

Japanese painted ferns truly light up the shade with silvery flashes from arching fronds that are detailed with burgundy to red stems. They're so popular that they were named the Perennial Plant Association's 2004 Perennial Plant of the Year. Their underground rhizomes system seems to creep out, producing small hedges of 12- to 18-inch-long (30.5 to 46 cm) fronds in a splayed-out, informal fashion that persists through the growing season.

CULTURE

Like its cousin the lady fern, the Japanese painted fern prefers moist, rich, well-drained soil in partial to full shade but can tolerate some sunlight. Morning sun is helpful in boosting the brightness of the leaf color.

PROPAGATION

Propagate division of clumps or grow from spores. It may self-sow in the garden, but spore-grown offspring do not come true and will show a lot of variation, with or without color.

NOTES

Japanese painted ferns naturally grow with variations in color. If you're buying a plant from a nursery, choose one that appeals the most to you. Selections with whiter leaf colors will seem brightest in the shade. Several named varieties, including 'Burgundy Lace', 'Pewter Lace', and 'Ursula's Red,' feature special coloration on the leaves or their stalks. The most exciting leaf colors are strongest in the spring, with fronds turning greener with hotter temperatures. This is a deciduous fern, so the quality of the fronds will decline as the season nears its end. Snip off old or spent fronds as they occur. The plants survive winter temperatures down to about –20 to –30°F (–29 to –34°C).

Eared Lady Fern

BOTANICAL NAME | *Athyrium oblitescens* (previously incorrectly identified as and called *A. otophorum*)

Eared lady fern represents a sort of bridge between the lady fern and the Japanese painted fern. Like the Japanese painted fern, it has burgundy- to raspberry-colored stems, but the frond colors are more subtle, starting out as a pale chartreuse or lime green that ages to a bluish, ashy medium green. As new fronds emerge throughout the growing season, the plant has an almost two-toned appearance. Like the lady fern, it grows in a tufted clump.

CULTURE

Grow this handsome 1- to 2-foot-tall (30.5 to 61 cm) fern in partial to full shade. Place it in well-drained soil that's kept moist but not wet. The leaves will appear to scorch—even in shade—and die if it doesn't get enough water. It tolerates most soil types if the drainage is good.

PROPAGATION

Propagate by division of clumps or grow from spores.

NOTES

The eared lady fern, native to eastern Asia, is likely to be one of the earliest of the lady ferns to emerge in spring. Its penchant for life extends its life in autumn, when it can persist well into frost, finally going dormant when frost and cold weather set in. Snip off fading fronds as they lose vigor. It easily survives winter soil temperatures of about -20 to -30°F (-29 to -34°C).

Alpine Water Fern (also called Little Hard Fern)

BOTANICAL NAME | *Blechnum penna-marina*

Spring is the season when the alpine water fern shines. Fronds just 4 to 8 inches (10 to 20 cm) tall emerge an unusual shade of salmon to coppery red, then turn glossy green before aging to rusty brown by fall and winter. This creeping fern is often used to fill crevices between rock walls or little-used paving stones, or as a short groundcover in moist areas. If you plant alpine water fern under trees or shrubs, be sure the branches are high enough to allow light to filter down to reach it on the ground.

CULTURE

Alpine water fern needs some morning sun or some filtered afternoon light to maintain its bright little fronds. It grows best in medium to high light, partial sun to partial shade, in a well-drained, acidic soil that's evenly moist to wet. It is somewhat forgiving of dry conditions once established.

PROPAGATION

Propagate by division of clumps; difficult to grow from spores.

NOTES

This is a rather tender fern, surviving winter temperatures only down to about 0 to 10°F (-18 to -12°C). It's native to parts of Chile, New Zealand, Australia, and some Pacific islands. The leaves are considered evergreen—snip off aged leaves when they no longer look fresh. As its name implies, the alpine water fern suits areas near ponds or boggy areas, where it will slowly colonize a space with stolons. It's considered one of the easier ferns to grow.

Hairy Lip Fern

BOTANICAL NAME | *Myriopteris lanosa (syn. Cheilanthes lanosa)*

Hairy lip fern is something of a unicorn among ferns: It tolerates sun and hot, dry conditions. It's a native of the Eastern and Midwestern United States, and its green, fuzzy fronds and dark brown stems are covered with dainty, woolly, hairlike scales for protection from situations that would fry most other ferns. Despite these great qualities, hairy lip fern performs best when it's not completely blasted with full sun from dawn to dusk. At 6 to 12 inches (15 to 30.5 cm) tall, it's no giant, but it does things most of the others can't.

CULTURE

Grow hairy lip fern in full sun to partial shade. It prefers its shallow roots grounded in excessively well-drained soil or loose, gritty rock with neutral to acidic pH. It also does well in a container planted with well-draining potting soil. Water sparingly but regularly.

PROPAGATION

Grow from spores or purchase plants. Do not remove plants from the wild. The plants may not survive transplantation and they are considered vulnerable, endangered, or extinct in some of the hairy lip fern's native ranges, although they are still ample worldwide.

NOTES

This deciduous fern with brown stems tolerates the cold down to about -10 to -20°F (-23 to -29°C). Grow it in a rock garden, in a trough garden, or in spaces between rock walls. In its native habitat, hairy lip fern is often found in shallow, dry soil in rocky conditions. This is one of the easiest xeric ferns to grow.

Fortune's Holly Fern (also called Japanese Holly Fern)

BOTANICAL NAME | *Cyrtomium fortunei*

The leaves on the fronds of Fortune's holly fern resemble those of holly shrubs. The large leaves on upright fronds emerge in spring with a bright, almost lime-green color, then age to a leathery medium green as the season progresses. This 1- to 2-foot-tall (30.5 to 61 cm) holly fern, native to temperate parts of Asia, is evergreen in the warmer areas of its growing range but loses its leaves in colder regions, where it survives down to about -5 to -10°F (-21 to -23°C).

CULTURE

Plant Fortune's holly fern in evenly moist, well-drained soil. If it's left in waterlogged soil, the roots can rot, especially in cold winters. Plant in partial to full shade. It does especially well in a location with morning sun and afternoon shade.

PROPAGATION

Grow from spores.

NOTES

This holly fern was named for Robert Fortune, a Scottish horticulturist who collected plants in China in the 1800s. Fortune's holly fern can easily be grown in containers, as well as in woodland areas. In some areas in Oregon and the Deep South, this fern has naturalized outside of gardens. Though Fortune's holly fern is not yet considered invasive, gardeners in those areas may want to consider this when making a fern choice.

Hay-Scented Fern

BOTANICAL NAME | *Dennstaedtia punctilobula*

This fern, when brushed or crushed by hand, emits a scent like freshly mown hay. It also tolerates more sun and drier conditions than most ferns, making it a good choice for areas that may span both shade and sunny spots. If you have a small garden, beware: This groundcover fern may become way too happy and take over your space. It's perfect for an area where you want easy-care coverage, such as the edge of a woodland that's sometimes in sun, sometimes in shade.

CULTURE

Hay-scented fern grows in almost any type of soil in full sun to partial shade. It likes moist, preferably acidic soil rich with humus, but can tolerate dry conditions. If it is grown in dry soil in a warm climate, even in shade, the quality of the fronds will decline by the end of summer. In sunnier, drier, and hotter conditions, the leaves will usually be smaller in size.

PROPAGATION

Propagate by division of clumps or grow from spores.

NOTES

The fine-textured foliage reaches 1 to 2 feet (30.5 to 61 cm) tall, emerging yellowish green in spring, then aging to a light green. This is a tough fern, a native of eastern North America that can survive winters that reach -30 to -40°F (-34 to -40°C). The plant goes dormant in winter, so clip off dead or dying fronds in late fall or early spring before new growth appears.

Golden-Scaled Male Fern

BOTANICAL NAME | *Dryopteris affinis* (syn. *D. borreri, D. pseudomas*)

The golden-scaled male fern shines in the spring when the fiddleheads (crosiers) emerge covered with bronzy yellow scales, as if rising from a vault of underground coins. The leaves on the fronds are yellowish green in spring, then become medium green as the season progresses. This native of Europe and parts of Asia is easy to grow, reaching 3 to 4 feet (91 to 122 cm) tall and wide at maturity.

CULTURE

Golden-scaled male fern is a bit more sun- and drought-tolerant than some ferns, but like most others, it grows best in rich, moist, well-drained soil in partial shade. It is tolerant of most soil pH levels. If you grow this fern in sunny locations with humid summers, provide extra water during dry periods.

PROPAGATION

Propagate by division of clumps or grow from spores.

NOTES

This robust fern is evergreen in warmer regions and semi-evergreen in the coldest regions where it can live. Fronds generally live about a year and a half before they start to decline. The golden scales persist throughout the lifespan of the fronds, lending it a second common name of golden shield fern. Feel |free to remove any fronds that look crispy or aged. Golden-scaled male fern survives winters to about -20 to -30°F (-29 to -34°C) and is a majestic addition to any garden. The complex of golden-scaled male fern that had been classified as *D. affinis* has been re-evaluated and some variations are now their own species. Don't be surprised if you find confusion in the listing of names.

Autumn Fern

BOTANICAL NAME | *Dryopteris erythrosora*

The autumn fern is beloved by many fern aficionados—I highly recommend it for any garden. The confounding part of its common name is that its fall coloration is brightest in the spring. Fronds emerge russet or coppery pink, then age to a shiny green for summer. By autumn, another hint of brownish red may return to the leaves. The fall color also is punctuated with red spore-producing sori on the undersides of the fronds. New fronds may shoot up throughout the growing season, lending interesting pink tones to any already established green growth.

CULTURE

Autumn fern prefers an average well-drained soil in partial to most shade, low to medium-high light. Keep the soil moist, especially during hot, dry summers, but not waterlogged. Too much moisture can rot the roots. Place autumn ferns in a wind-protected spot.

PROPAGATION

Propagate by division of clumps, spores, or rhizome cuttings.

NOTES

Autumn fern, a native of Japan and eastern Asia, reaches about 1 ½ to 2 ½ feet (46 to 76 cm) tall and is cold-hardy down to about -10 to -20°F (-23 to -29°C). It is considered evergreen in most of its range and semi-evergreen in the coldest regions. Snip off any aged fronds to maintain a tidy appearance. The spring color of the cultivar 'Brilliance' is considered redder and longer lasting than the species.

Male Fern

BOTANICAL NAME | *Dryopteris filix-mas*

The shape and form of a mature male fern has been compared to that of a badminton shuttlecock, with the fronds reaching about 2 to 4 feet (61 to 122 cm) tall and wide. This sturdy fern, native to temperate areas of the Northern Hemisphere, is cold hardy down to about -20 to -30°F (-29 to -34°C). The rhizomes are less aggressive in growth than some other ferns, making it easier to contain in small spaces.

CULTURE

Like many ferns, male ferns prefer rich, well-drained soil in partial to full shade. Don't allow the soil to dry out completely—especially during hot summers—but avoid keeping the soil waterlogged, as too much moisture can rot the roots. If possible, site male ferns where they are protected from strong winds that can damage the fronds.

PROPAGATION

Propagate by division of clumps or grow from spores.

NOTES

The male fern is believed to have gotten its common name because it is so robust and vigorous. It was initially believed to be the male form of the lady fern. However, the two plants are genetically different. Male fern comes in more than fifty attractive alternate forms, including those with crisped, crested, forked, and dwarf variations. It is similar to, and often confused with *D. affinis,* but is deciduous. Snip off old fronds when they lose vigor.

Marginal Wood Fern

BOTANICAL NAME | *Dryopteris marginalis*

Native to North America, the marginal wood fern is common in woodlands and rocky ledges and bluffs. The common name describes the location of the spore cases, which are found on the margins of the leaflets. The marginal wood fern also stays in bounds, typically growing as a single 1- to 3-foot-tall (30.5 to 91 cm) specimen. Plant multiples to create a nice grouping.

CULTURE

Marginal wood fern prefers average, well-drained soil and a location in partial to full shade. Though it has some drought and sun tolerance, it prefers moist, rich soil that's not waterlogged. Shelter this fern from high winds, which can damage the fronds.

PROPAGATION

Propagate by division of clumps or grow from spores.

NOTES

The handsome evergreen fronds have a leathery texture and a bluish cast and look good through the winter, even in its northernmost range where temperatures can dip to -30 to -40°F (-34 to -40°C). By spring, however, they may no longer look fresh, so feel free to snip them off to allow the new growth to shine. In the United States, it performs best east of the Rocky Mountains. Besides its use in woodland gardens, planting masses of these ferns can help stabilize dry, shaded slopes.

Scouringrush (also called Evergreen Scouring Rush)

BOTANICAL NAME | *Equisetum hyemale*

Horsetail was once considered a fern ally but has since been classified as a true fern. Horsetail reproduces using spores, but it also spreads via rhizomes so aggressively that gardeners often wish they hadn't planted it. Even a small bit of rhizome left in the ground will sprout a new plant, so it is difficult to eradicate once established. However, used with proper barriers, horsetail is an asset to contemporary, Asian, or midcentury landscape designs. The handsome deep green, jointed, hollow stems reach 2 to 4 feet (61 to 122 cm) tall and offer a unique vertical accent to the garden.

CULTURE

Horsetail rhizomes quickly fill whatever moist space is allowed. Consider planting in an impervious pot with no drainage holes—it can grow in up to 4 inches (10 cm) of water—or in a pot where the soil is constantly moist. Use soil barriers if you plant it in the ground. It grows in full sun to full shade.

PROPAGATION

Propagate from rhizome cuttings or grow from spores.

NOTES

Horsetail is an interesting living fossil that originated approximately 350 million years ago. Because of its high silica content, indigenous people used horsetails as scouring brushes. It is evergreen and survives winter temperatures as low as -30 to -40°F (-34 to -40°C).

Oak Fern

BOTANICAL NAME | *Gymnocarpium dryopteris*

The oak fern is a charming, slow-growing perennial found around the Northern Hemisphere. Its rhizomes creep slowly, so it's easy to control and makes a beautiful ground cover. Rarely reaching more than 1 foot (30.5 cm) tall, it sports delicate-looking, triangular, horizontal fronds that emerge in spring. The foliage starts out a light apple green color that ages to a medium green. Oak ferns produce new fronds throughout the growing season. Oddly, despite the common name, oak ferns are not found growing near oak trees, nor do their fronds resemble oak leaves.

CULTURE

Oak fern grows best in well-drained, moist soil in partial to full shade. It will tolerate sand or clay soils as long as they don't dry out completely. Offer supplemental watering during droughts.

PROPAGATION

Propagate by division of clumps, from rhizome cuttings, or grow from spores.

NOTES

The crushed fronds of oak ferns were used in earlier times to repel mosquitoes and treat bites. This deciduous fern's good looks are likely to fade as the growing season progresses, especially in areas of hot, dry summers. Feel free to snip off any dying fronds for a tidier appearance. A boon to Northern gardeners, oak fern is a truly tough plant that survives winters as cold as -40 to -50°F (-40 to 46°C).

Netted Chain Fern

BOTANICAL NAME | *Lorinseria areolata* (syn. *Woodwardia areolata*)

Netted chain fern, native to eastern North America, is a swamp- and bog-loving fern. Take a good close look at its wide green leaflets to see the netted veining pattern. This fern has separate sterile and fertile fronds. The other part of the common name comes from fertile fronds that carry spores arranged in chainlike rows. This 18- to 24-inch-tall (46 to 61 cm) fern can multiply into large colonies in wet ground, thanks to its rampant rhizomes.

CULTURE

Grow netted chain fern in a bog, pondside, or in rich, well-drained soils in partial to full shade. It can take more sun if the soil is kept consistently moist. Moisture is key to keeping this fern alive.

PROPAGATION

Propagate by dividing clumps if they're large enough, from rhizome cuttings, or grow from spores.

NOTES

This fern is similar in appearance to the sensitive fern (*Onoclea sensibilis*, page 161). However, sensitive ferns are more common and generally 12 to 24 inches (30.5 to 61 cm) taller, with smooth leaflets and beaded fertile fronds. Netted chain fern is deciduous, shedding its leaves by the end of the season. Clip off old or dead fronds to make way for the following spring's bronze-colored growth. It is a tough perennial, surviving winters that can reach -30 to -40°F (-34 to -40°C). It's a great plant to naturalize in a boggy semi-shaded area.

Ostrich Fern

BOTANICAL NAME | *Matteuccia struthiopteris* (syn. *M. pensylvanica*, *Struthiopteris pensylvanica*, *Pteretis nodulosa*)

Ostrich fern is a happy-go-lucky, super-hardy perennial, ready to romp through as much space as you can give it in the cooler regions of its native North America. It is most exuberant in moist shade, but also growns in wet areas. This tendency to run and form massive colonies makes it difficult to contain in small gardens. It's also a monster: The fronds can reach up to 6 feet (1.8 m) tall when it grows in moist and cool conditions in the wild. Ostrich fern produces tight fiddleheads that are often harvested and cooked—they should not be consumed raw—as a spring delicacy. When left to grow to maturity, the huge, feathery fronds resemble the plumes of its namesake flightless bird.

CULTURE

Grow ostrich ferns in moist, rich, well-drained soil with almost any pH. Don't be surprised if the fronds of the ostrich fern, which look so magnificent in spring, decline during dry spells. They don't grow well in hot areas. The fronds can easily be beaten down by wind and hail.

PROPAGATION

Propagate by division of clumps, by seperating new plants formed on stolons, or grow from spores.

NOTES

This is a deciduous fern, so even if the fronds maintain their appearance over the growing season, expect them to die back in time for winter dormancy. The separate fertile fronds are brown and woody looking; they persist through the winter and provide decorative interest. It survives winters down to -30 to -40°F (-34 to -40°C).

Sensitive Fern

BOTANICAL NAME | *Onoclea sensibilis*

No, the sensitive fern doesn't quiver and close when you touch it. The common name comes from this deciduous fern's quick response to frost. It immediately shifts colors from green to brown. Once you learn about them, it's easy to identify sensitive ferns because of the distinctive profiles of the fronds. The nonfertile fronds carry rather large serrated medium green leaves that don't emerge in spring until the danger of frost has passed. The fertile fronds don't bear leaves at all, but resemble stalks with small, dark brown beads. These beadlike structures hold the spores made in the summer and release them the following winter, giving this fern another common name: bead fern.

CULTURE

Sensitive ferns prefer to grow in partial to full shade but tolerate full sun if given enough moisture. Shelter plants from strong winds. In the wild, they grow well in disturbed areas along wetlands. The rhizomes can multiply quickly in ideal conditions, so control them quickly if they're getting out of bounds.

PROPAGATION

Propagate by division of clumps, from rhizome cuttings, or grow from spores.

NOTES

Sensitive ferns, native in many cooler parts of the Northern Hemisphere, appear to have originated millions of years ago, based on fossil imprints. It reaches 2 feet (61 cm) tall and wide and survives winters down to -20 to -40°F (-29 to -40°C).

Royal Fern

BOTANICAL NAME | *Osmunda regalis*

The royal fern is a regal addition to any shade garden. It has a distinctive appearance, with fleshy, rounded leaflets that more closely resemble members of the pea family or black locust trees (*Robinia*) instead of ferns. The fertile fronds of the royal fern are located on upright brown fronds that give it another common name: flowering fern.

CULTURE

Royal fern thrives on moisture and grows well in boggy areas or near wooded streams and ponds. With constant moisture and partial shade, it can reach 6 feet (1.8 m) tall or more. Despite its love of water, the royal fern is more tolerant of sun than many other ferns and can be drought tolerant. More sun and less moisture, however, produces smaller plants. In warmer climates, plant royal ferns in partial to full shade.

PROPAGATION

Propagate by division of clumps or grow from spores.

NOTES

Royal fern has two varieties, one native to Europe and Asia, the other native to North America. The European variety, *Osmunda regalis* var. *regalis* is usually larger and more robust, has more leathery leaflets, and typically stays green until freezing weather, whereas the North American one, *Osmunda regalis* var. *spectabilis*, tends to be smaller and more slender in appearance and turns yellow as cold approaches. Both slow-growing ferns grow in many parts of the world, surviving winters that reach from -30 to -40°F (-34 to -40°C), possibly colder.

Cinnamon Fern

BOTANICAL NAME | *Osmundastrum cinnamomeum* (syn. *Osmunda cinnamomea*)

The cinnamon fern, perhaps unfortunately, does not smell like cinnamon. But the rust-colored, spore-bearing, fertile fronds certainly mimic the color as they stand like stiff and slender soldiers among the 2- to 4-foot (61 to 122 cm), vase-shaped, sterile green fronds. In the fall, the sterile fronds turn from green to yellow before these deciduous ferns go dormant for the winter. By summer, the fertile fronds will have released their spores and died back. The plant can survive winter temperatures down to -30 to -40°F (-34 to -40°C).

CULTURE

Grow cinnamon ferns in moist, well-drained neutral to acid soil in partial to full shade. Dappled or filtered shade is best. In its native habitat, it likes to grow in wetlands, making it a good choice to grow along ponds, streams, and water gardens. If grown in hot, dry shade without supplemental water, this fern's fronds will quickly begin a downward slide toward dormancy, by late summer if not earlier.

PROPAGATION

Propagate by division of clumps or grow from spores.

NOTES

The cinnamon in the common name refers to the dense upright clusters of cinnamon-colored spores. The dense bases of the ferns with old roots are sometimes used as a component in orchid potting mixes but should not be harvested for such purposes. Cinnamon fern is not overly aggressive.

Narrow Beech Fern (Beech Fern, Long Beech Fern)

BOTANICAL NAME | *Phegopteris connectilis (syn. Thelypteris phegopteris)*

The narrow beech fern not only has narrow leaves on its triangular fronds, it has a narrow range in which it can live, too. Native to northern parts of North America, Europe, and Asia, the narrow beech fern is hardy enough to survive winters of -40 to -50°F (-40 to -46°F). But it can't stand the heat and humidity of the American South and won't be happy much south of the Mason-Dixon Line or in the heat of the American Southwest.

CULTURE

Narrow beech ferns grow best in moist, well-drained, rich, acidic soil in partial to full shade. In native areas, it thrives in cool woodlands and along streambanks where there's a steady source of moisture. For the best coloration—a pale green in spring and early summer—it should grow where some dappled or filtered light can come through.

PROPAGATION

Propagate from rhizome cutting or grow from spores. Never collect narrow beech fern from the wild.

NOTES

Narrow beech fern reaches just 9 to 18 inches (23 to 46 cm) tall, spreading very slowly from its tiny, creeping rhizomes. This deciduous fern is also known to be epipetric, meaning it can grow on or out of rocks, though it prefers to grow in moist soil. This is a fern to best enjoy in the wild, as it is rare in garden cultivation and endangered in the western portions of its United States habitat.

Japanese Beech Fern

BOTANICAL NAME | *Phegopteris decursive-pinnata* (syn. *Thelypteris decursive-pinnata*)

One American nursery called the Japanese beech fern "one of the best landscape ferns we've tried over the years," and it's easy to see why. This sturdy fern is compact yet noticeable at 1 to 2 feet (30.5 to 61 cm) tall. The short rhizomes of its tidy clumps are well behaved and slow to run, but easily controlled if they spread too much. The dark green fronds stay upright, then arch slightly. A bit of a breeze reveals their light green undersides.

CULTURE

Grow Japanese beech fern, like most ferns, in moist, rich, well-drained soil. It can grow in full shade but is likely to stay smaller and grow more slowly than in areas where it gets a bit of sunshine each day. It tolerates heat and some sun but needs supplemental moisture in both cases. The best site has plenty of moisture in bright shade that receives morning or late afternoon sun.

PROPAGATION

Propagate by seperating new plants produced on short runners or grow from spores.

NOTES

This fern is winter hardy down to -20 to -30°F (-29 to -34°C). It is deciduous but remains green until a hard frost; it may remain evergreen in warmer regions. Its ability to tolerate both heat and cold weather makes it a good choice for most areas except the Far North.

Licorice Fern (Sweet Root Fern)

BOTANICAL NAME | *Polypodium glycyrrhiza*

The licorice fern is a bit of a surprise. Its botanical name describes a couple of this fern's many unusual qualities. *Polypodium* means "many footed," so instead of originating all its fronds from one central spot, licorice fern grows its fronds at random points along its creeping rhizomes. The word *glycyrrhiza* refers to the sweet (*glykys* from Greek) licorice flavor of its rhizomes (*rhiza*, meaning root). Indigenous peoples used these tasty roots for flavoring and medicines. Another interesting trait: Licorice fern is dormant during the summer but begins growing leathery green fronds again from early fall through spring in the temperate and tropical climates where it is native. Finally, it is epiphytic, meaning its roots don't need to be grown in soil but can cling to vertical surfaces, such as moss-covered rocks or trees.

CULTURE

Grow licorice fern in partial to full shade. It will grow in moist soil but can clamber up trees, especially maples, or rock faces on which moss grows naturally. The moisture-retaining moss helps to cool and protect its shallow root system.

PROPAGATION

Propagate from rhizome cuttings or grow from spores.

NOTES

This unusual, 1- to 2-foot–tall (30.5 to 61 cm) fern is native to the Pacific Northwest and prefers areas with cool, moist summers and warm, wet winters. It grows only where winter temperatures dip no lower than -10°F (-23°C).

Christmas Fern

BOTANICAL NAME | *Polystichum acrostichoides*

They may not get decorated with ornaments and lights, but Christmas fern fronds stay evergreen, even when lying flat under a heap of snow. The 1- to 2-foot (30.5 to 61 cm), leathery green fronds are often used in holiday floral arrangements. This hardy fern grows in many places, surviving winters with temperatures down to -30 to -40°F (-34 to -40°C). It grows mainly east of the Rocky Mountains in the United States. A relative, the Western sword fern *Polystichum munitum* (see page 169), fills the same role west of the Rockies.

CULTURE

Grow Christmas fern in rich, well-drained soil in partial to full shade. Plant the crown of this fern at an angle to prevent water or snowmelt from collecting inside and rotting the plant. Though they thrive with good soil and adequate moisture, keep once established, Christmas ferns can survive in drought conditions in clay soil or rubble and tolerate deeper shade. Snip off old fronds in spring before new ones emerge.

PROPAGATION

Propagate by division of clumps or grow from spores.

NOTES

The size of the clumps increases over time, but although this fern grows rhizomes, the roots don't spread much beyond one to three clumps. Each clump's fronds rise from a single point, growing in a circular pattern. When planted in masses on a shady hillside, Christmas ferns are helpful in controlling soil erosion.

OUTDOOR FERN PROFILES

Makino's Holly Fern

BOTANICAL NAME | *Polystichum makinoi*

Makino's holly fern is something of a darling in the horticulture world, with good reason: It's a real looker. Satiny to glossy olive-green, arching fronds adorn sturdy, stiff stems covered with attractive dark brown scales. The 1- to 2-foot-tall (30.5 to 61 cm) tidy clumps seem more elegant and prepossessing than some other types of ferns. It's a great garden choice used alone as a specimen or massed for effect. It also performs well in a container located in a shady spot. In the garden, its lacy texture works well as a foil against shade plants with broad leaves. Pair its olive color against deep green or variegated gold-green foliage.

CULTURE

Makino's holly fern prefers to grow in rich, moist, well-drained soil, but can tolerate clay or sandy soils. It tolerates hot, dry summer weather but fares better if offered supplemental water during periods of drought. It grows in partial to full shade.

PROPAGATION

Propagate by division of clumps or grow from spores.

NOTES

This Asian native is considered evergreen. The previous year's growth will decline after new fronds appear, so clip back the old fronds in late winter to early spring. Makino's holly fern survives winters that reach as cold as -10 to -20°F (-23 to -29°C).

Western Sword Fern

BOTANICAL NAME | *Polystichum munitum*

If they were forged into actual swords of human size, the individual serrated leaflets of the western sword fern would indeed be mighty. But even with fronds, this fern is a mighty presence in the shade of natural and cultivated gardens in the Western United States, the Pacific Northwest, and adjacent areas of Canada. It refuses to grow well east of the Rocky Mountains but its relative the Christmas fern, *Polystichum acrostichoides*, takes over from there. (See page 167). Evergreen clumps of fronds that grow from about 4 feet (1.2 m) to nearly 6 feet (1.8 m) long make this a fern to reckon with.

CULTURE

Grow the Western sword fern in a woodland setting in partial to full shade, where it has plenty of room to spread out. In locations with more sun, the plant grows more upright, with shorter fronds. It grows best in rich, well-drained, acidic soil. This fern survives occasional drought but needs supplemental water to look its best. It prefers cooler weather and consistent moisture.

PROPAGATION

Propagate by division of clumps or grow from spores.

NOTES

Western sword fern survives winter temperatures down to about 0 to -10°F (-18 to -23°C). Individual fronds have a lifespan of about 1 to 2 years. When new growth appears in spring, check the old fronds. Remove any that are declining in appearance, unless you want them to remain to decompose and augment the soil.

Tassel Fern

BOTANICAL NAME | *Polystichum polyblepharum*

Spring becomes more fun when you grow a tassel fern. After the emerging crosiers start growing, they bend over backwards so the unfolding leaflets at the tip resemble tassels. By the time the 1- to 2-foot (30.5 to 61 cm) fronds unfurl completely, the tassel effect is gone, leaving a tidy clump of glossy, dark green foliage that is evergreen. Tassel ferns are a must-have for gardeners.

CULTURE

Grow tassel ferns in rich, moist well-drained soil in partial to full shade. You'll get the best performance in an area of dappled shade, or with morning sun and afternoon shade. When planting, tilt the crown of the rhizome at an angle instead of straight up. This helps prevent water from collecting in the crown and rotting the plant. Crown rot is most common during the winter in poorly drained soil.

PROPAGATION

Propagate by division of clumps or grow from spores.

NOTES

This well-behaved fern hails from Korea and Japan. It is hardy in winters with temperatures down to -10 to -20°F (-23 to -29°C). It also does well in a container as a large houseplant, or in a shaded area of the garden. The stems of tassel fern are covered with a multitude of brown hairs, which explains the *polyblepharum* part of its botanical name—it means "many eyelashes."

Soft Shield Fern

BOTANICAL NAME | *Polystichum setiferum* (syn. *P. angulare*)

It's not entirely clear where the soft shield fern gets its common name. *Setiferum* means "bristled," and *polystichum* roughly translates as "with bristles," referring to the soft bristly tips on the leaflets. In any case, this handsome fern graces a home garden with 2- to 3-foot (61 to 91 cm) arching green fronds.

CULTURE

Grow this European native in rich, moist, well-drained soil in partial to full shade. You'll get the best performance in an area of dappled shade or with morning sun and afternoon shade. Too much sun causes the foliage to turn yellow. When planting, tilt the crown of the rhizome at an angle instead of straight up to prevent water from collecting in the crown and rotting the plant. Crown rot is most common during the winter in poorly drained soil. It will tolerate short periods of drought but should have supplemental water if possible.

PROPAGATION

Propagate by division of clumps. The straight species can be grown from spores. The various cultivars don't usually come true from spores, but some of them produce proliferations (bulbils) on their fronds and can be propagated that way.

NOTES

Soft shield fern is evergreen or semievergreen, depending on the climate, with individual fronds living for 9 to 15 months. Once spent, they'll stay attached to the rhizome unless you choose to clip them off in the interest of tidiness. Nearly 400 varieties were named during the Victorian fern craze, a number of which are still prized and available.

Arborvitae Fern or Braun's Spikemoss

BOTANICAL NAME | *Selaginella braunii*

Selaginella braunii masquerades as a fern, but it is really a spikemoss, a member of a group of plants called lycophytes or fern allies. Lycophytes, which were outlined in Chapter 1, are nonflowering plants that reproduce via spores. Arborvitae fern looks like a cross between a fern and a dwarf conifer. Its upright green, lacy fronds resemble the foliage of an arborvitae evergreen. Grow it for its unusual foliage, which adds texture in a shade garden planted with broadleaved plants such as hostas.

CULTURE

This 6- to 18-inch (15 to 46 cm) charmer grows from very slowly spreading rhizomes, forming a 2-foot-wide (61 cm) clump in about 3 years. It prefers moist, well-drained soil in partial to full shade, although it can tolerate drier soil once it is established. As with other ferns, offer supplemental water during periods of drought.

PROPAGATION

Propagate by division of clumps.

NOTES

Arborvitae fern's foliage is evergreen in warmer climates, semi-evergreen and bronze colored in cooler regions, and may turn brown in the coldest areas. The fronds, late to emerge in spring, are a bright green color, then turn a darker green in fall. This plant is not a fan of cold regions, though it will survive in winters that reach 0 to -10°F (-18 to -23°C).

New York Fern

BOTANICAL NAME | *Thelypteris noveboracensis* (syn. *Parathelypteris noveboracensis*)

Start spreading the news: The New York fern is an excellent spreading groundcover if you have lots of space. Its 1- to 2-foot (30.5 to 61 cm) lacy green fronds are readily identifiable by their distinctive shapes. They are tapered at both ends and wider in the middle.

CULTURE

The New York fern is a member of the marsh fern family and loves moist to wet sites. It grows in dappled sunlight to partial shade in acidic soils. It especially likes to grow below breaks in a forest canopy, where it can get a bit of direct sunshine each day, but not all day. It will tolerate some sun if it's kept moist enough. It will deteriorate well before its normal fall dormancy if it gets too much sun or is left in drought conditions too long. Plant it in areas where it is protected from strong wind.

PROPAGATION

Propagate by division of clumps, from rhizome cuttings, or grow from spores.

NOTES

Given its ideal growing situation (acidic soil, partial sun, plenty of moisture), the New York fern aggressively takes over, forming a dense groundcover. If you plant it under trees, beware: Its roots emit a chemical toxic to some trees, especially wild black cherry (*Prunus serotina*). This deciduous fern achieves yellow fall color before it dies back to the ground. Its rhizomes survive winter temperatures in the range of -20 to -30°F (-29 to -34°C).

Blunt-Lobed Woodsia

BOTANICAL NAME | *Woodsia obtusa*

Take a good look at the lower leaflets of this blunt-lobed wood fern, and you'll see how it got its common name. Instead of coming to a point, each leaflet has a rounded edge, as if someone had trimmed it to fit into a tiny oblong space. This easy-to-grow American native is also known as the cliff fern, giving a clue where it likes to grow. Its dainty stature—just 6 to 18 inches (15 to 46 cm) tall—and lacy green fronds make it a good choice for tucking into a small space of a woodland or rock garden. However, it may be difficult to find for sale, as few commercial sources propagate the plant.

CULTURE

Blunt-lobed woodsia grows in partial to full shade in moist, well-drained soils. It will grow among acidic or calcareous rocks and grows easily in the garden. It can't tolerate wet feet.

PROPAGATION

Propagate by division of clumps, from rhizome cuttings, or grow from spores.

NOTES

Blunt-lobed woodsia survives winters as cold as -20 to -30°F (-29 to -34°C). The leaves are deciduous, so feel free to snip off any aging or dead fronds by spring to allow new growth to shine. Woodsias are named after English architect, botanist, and author Joseph Woods (1776–1864).

Holly Fern Woodsia

BOTANICAL NAME | *Woodsia polystichoides*

This wood fern technically is not a holly fern, but gets its name because its leaflets are shaped like those of the holly ferns. It is one of the first ferns to emerge in spring, unfurling pale green fronds. Arching green and hairy fronds grow to 12 inches (30.5 cm) or less, making it a small charmer suitable for many locations, including rock gardens.

CULTURE

Grow holly fern woodsia in moist, well-drained soil. It is one of those rare ferns that prefers to grow in some sun. Full sun is too much, but it doesn't want to live in full shade, either. In areas with hot summers, plant holly fern woodsia in at least partial shade, and give it supplemental water during periods of drought.

PROPAGATION

Propagate by division of clumps or grow from spores.

NOTES

This Asian native is deciduous, dropping its leaves in autumn. Feel free to snip off any dead or dying fronds so the new spring growth can shine the following season. It is winter hardy where winter temperatures reach -20 to -30°F (-29 to -34°C). The small size of holly fern woodsia makes it easily to grow in a container, kept moist in a location that is both sunny and shady enough to keep it happy.

| CHAPTER 5 |

Do-It-Yourself
Crafting with Ferns

NOW THAT YOU'VE LEARNED ALL ABOUT FERNS and how to select which ones to grow, it's time to let your creative juices flow. The following pages are filled with fun, fresh, and inspiring ways to display your new fronds. These DIY projects allow you to express your own unique style as you design each individual piece to complement your personal space.

For all the following projects, please source plants responsibly. Never dig plants or harvest fronds from the wild. Purchase plants from reputable sources, or swap with friends. Use fronds from your own collection of houseplants and garden plants or those of friends, or purchase fronds from florists. Take care collecting, even on your own property. You might just be the lucky one to have a rare or endangered species growing in your backyard! Bottom line: Don't collect anything without permission from proper authorities.

Establishing a Terrarium

Terrariums are essentially miniature greenhouses. A true terrarium is fully enclosed and basically self-sustaining once it establishes, whereas open terrariums require regular checking, yet still provide the benefits of a more nurturing environment than an open, exposed setting. When it's completed, place your terrarium in a bright location, avoiding any direct sun, which will cook your plants. Ideal containers should be made of clear glass to allow enough light for your plants to grow. A true terrarium will have a base of potting soil in which the plants are actually planted and will need some type of lid to create a closed micro-environment. Containers of all types abound—the possibilities are limited only by your creativity. Shop discount stores, craft stores, and garage sales, and look for fish tanks and other items you can repurpose.

Once you've chosen your container, make sure the plants will fit inside. Ideally, choose miniature plants that can survive indefinitely and won't outgrow the space. The trending popularity of fairy gardens has helped make miniature plants more readily available. If you opt to use smaller versions of species that grow larger (young plants, rooted cuttings, small divisions, and sporelings), you will have more trimming and maintenance to do as time goes on, and eventually the ferns will outgrow the space and you will need to replant. Plan out your design before you begin the project.

I simply love the look of a terrarium, and they are so much fun to make. It is very easy to see why they were such popular features during the Victorian fern craze.

WHAT YOU'LL NEED

→ A clean glass container with a lid. A wide opening at the top is the easiest to work with.

→ A few large stones. I use stones about 1 to 1½ inches (2.5 to 3.8 cm) long.

→ A piece of window screening. I prefer fiberglass, as it is nonreactive and very flexible.

→ Scissors.

→ Coarse-grade charcoal.

→ Terrarium potting mix.

→ Plants. The number of plants used and their pot sizes will be based on the size of your container.

→ A funnel or paper tube. If your opening is too small to scoop soil into place, you will need a funnel for filling the terrarium with soil.

→ Terrarium planting tools. Buy some or make your own: tongs, rake or cultivator (fork), scraper (knife), shovel (spoon), tamper (empty spool of thread), duster (paintbrush).

→ Watering can. A long, narrow spout is ideal. A turkey baster makes an acceptable substitute.

→ If you prefer to wear gloves, I recommend latex or nitrile gloves. Most other types of gloves are too bulky for small potting jobs.

STEPS

1 | Place your stones in the bottom of your container, creating a reservoir for any excess water. Hint: Don't drop the stones, or you may break the glass! Next, cut a piece of screen and place it over the stones. The screen should be the size and shape of the entire bottom, with a little extra to reach up the sides.

2 | Scoop some charcoal into your hand and place a ½-inch (13 mm) layer over the screening. Hint: Charcoal is very dusty; don't stir it up! You can moisten it a little to reduce dust. I recommend wearing gloves and a dust mask if you're very sensitive.

3 | With your design already planned, start adding some soil. I prefer to contour the soil for a very natural look that changes as you view it from different sides. It's best to make the high point on the outside. If you choose to keep your soil level, create interest with varying heights of plants and by adding rocks and wood.

4 | Begin planting. Start with the plant that will be the tallest and at the highest soil line. I prefer an asymmetrical planting, and often place the biggest plant off center. In this case, my fern was just a small division and didn't have a rootball. I simply brought the soil up to the final desired level and tucked in the rhizome and about 1 inch (2.5 cm) of the stem base, as this is how the plant was growing previously.

5 | Continue working outward from the high point and prep the next plant. Spread your pointer and middle fingers apart and place them over the top of the pot and around the base of the plant. Turn the pot over, and with your other hand gently shake or tap the plant out of its pot. Gently massage and loosen the soil around the top edge, sides, and bottom.

6 | Add more soil as needed and create a planting hole to bring the second plant up to the desired level. Place rootball in planting pocket.

7 | With one hand, hold the fronds out of the way and add more soil with your other hand. Using your miniature shovel, fill in soil around the rootball. Then, use your miniature tamper to firm the soil all around the rootball. Always make sure the original soil line of the rootball is even with the new surrounding soil. You don't want it deeper, burying the leaves. Nor do you want it higher, exposing the roots. Also, smooth out the surrounding soil as you go, maintaining an even grade.

8 | Continue working outward. Prepare the third plant and use the miniature shovel to dig a hole and place the next plant in its pocket. Fill around the rootball with soil as needed, and firm in place. Repeat with the fourth plant.

9 | Add more soil as needed using a tube or funnel. Fill and firm around the rootball. Then finish planting any remaining plants.

10 | Use a miniature rake to smooth and give a final grade to the soil and use a miniature duster or paintbrush to carefully brush off any soil from the fronds. Also use it to clean off soil from the inside of the glass.

11 | Water in each individual plant sparingly. Check carefully over the next few weeks and adjust moisture levels if needed. The stone reservoir at the bottom should never be so full of water that it reaches up to the screen line. Put the lid on your terrarium and enjoy!

Finished planting includes *Psilotum nudum*, *Adiantum microphyllum* 'Little Lady', *Hemionitis arifolia*, and *Selaginella kraussiana* 'Aurea'.

When it comes to terrariums, watering should be done carefully and sparingly. Resist making the soil too wet, because it is very difficult to remove excess water. For the first few weeks, watch carefully as your terrarium establishes. If the soil is too wet, or there is excessive condensation (water collecting inside the glass), you may need to loosen or open the lid to let it dry out a little. Conversely, if the soil is too dry and there is insufficient humidity, you may need to add a little more water. Getting the moisture balance right can be a bit tricky and may take up to a few weeks, but once it stabilizes properly your terrarium will basically sustain itself and will only need to be checked periodically. Remember, however, that open terrariums will have to be checked regularly and will require water more frequently.

Additional decorative touches are optional and personal. If you have not planted a living groundcover, you may prefer to top the soil with a mulch of small pebbles, miniature orchid bark chips, or moss. For a more natural look, you can also add larger decorative rocks and twigs, or small branchlets. Many people like to add other touches, such as colorful glass chips or sand. Little Buddhas, gnomes, and fairies are also very popular figurines. Create your own settings using miniature furniture, tools, animals, and other props. There are many to choose from.

Creative Terrarium Variations

1. AN OPEN TERRARIUM. Remove your fern from its pot. Place in the bottom of glass container and cover entire rootball with extra soil, letting it spread out and around the bottom. If desired, you can cover the exposed soil with some moistened moss. Alternatively, you can simply place a potted fern in the container. Shown here is *Nephrolepis exaltata* 'Fluffy Ruffles'.

2. AN AQUARIUM. Use an aquatic fern to create an "aquatic terrarium" in a covered container. It is best to use small, clean gravel, stones, and similar material for these plantings. Source plants and stone at local pet stores or online. Add water as needed. Shown below and opposite are *Bolbitis heteroclita* and *Microsorum pteropus*.

3. A CLOCHE TERRARIUM. This type of terrarium consists of a flat base with a glass cover or cloche. Make sure your plant is well watered. Remove the plant from its pot and gently loosen the soil. Place your plant in the center of a shallow saucer (make sure it fits inside the base and cover) and gently press as much moist soil around the rootball as you can, filling the saucer. Cover the entire soil surface and saucer with moist moss (use sheet moss or long-fiber sphagnum moss). Cover with glass cloche. hown here: *Selaginella erythropus.*

4. A SAUCER TERRARIUM. This is like the cloche terrarium on the left with a flat base and a glass cover that fits over the top. Here, instead of a single plant, I've made a mixed garden. Ideally, the container should be the same depth as the biggest rootball. Use a very deep saucer or repurpose a plastic takeout food container for the job, as I did here. Three different plants make for a nice grouping. Plant them together in the container, filling in around them with moist soil and firming around their rootballs. No need to leave a watering lip. Cover the entire container with moist moss (use sheet moss or long-fiber sphagnum moss). If your container is decorative, there's no need to cover it, but if you prefer, cover with a glass cloche. Shown here: *Nephrolepis exaltata* 'Emina', *Selaginella uncinata*, and *Pellaea rotundifolia.*

Planting a Vertical Garden

Vertical gardening is a new trend. Expanding onto vertical surfaces maximizes space and adds a whole new dimension to gardening. As living and working space increasingly comes at a premium, growing upward is a natural progression. Various types of kits are available to make a green wall: fabric planting pouches, metal or plastic trays, units with irrigation systems, and setups with decorative covers or frames. They can be filled with a growing medium (e.g., soilless mix) and planted directly, or can simply hold potted plants. Green walls are wonderful additions indoors and out. Choose a style that will work in your situation.

In interior settings, waterproof planters that have catch basins are most appropriate. No one wants water running onto furniture, carpeting, or wooden floors. Look at your indoor environment—light and temperature—and choose plants suited to the amount of light your living wall will receive. Also, make sure your plants are compatible in their water needs.

Outdoors, you can use ready-made products or be creative and make your own. A very popular and rather easy DIY green wall can be made by repurposing a wooden pallet. Choose plants suitable to your climate and general growing conditions, selecting those that will grow with the amount of light they will get. Note that when making an outdoor living wall, it is important to understand that plants growing above ground are more exposed, and therefore more vulnerable. They typically dry out faster and are more susceptible to temperature fluctuations. Watch your watering, and make sure that the types you choose can withstand the additional cold and/or heat they will be exposed to.

Living walls beautify our surroundings and improve our environments. They bring us joy and have a positive effect on our physical and mental well-being.

➻ Vertical container. I chose this kit by GroVert. It consists of a plastic planter with a decorative wooden frame. In the back, it has a catch basin at the bottom to prevent dripping. You can also get a basin that fits at the top (also on the back) that you fill with water for ease of watering. It's ready and easy to use. Some types of vertical containers could also hold potted plants, if you prefer that method.

➻ Standard fern potting mix, enough to fill the planting pockets at most.

➻ Ten 4-inch (10 cm) potted ferns. The number of plants used and their pot sizes will be based on the planter you use. The soil in the pots should be moist. If they are dry, give them a drink, preferably the day before.

➻ Decorative moss. I prefer preserved Spanish moss for this.

➻ If you prefer to wear gloves, I recommend latex or nitrile gloves. Most other types of gloves are too bulky for small potting jobs.

STEPS

1 | This kit from GroVert comes with all the hardware to hang it on the wall. Decide where you want to hang it and attach the necessary hardware to the wall according to the included instructions. After your planter is completed, you'll simply line it up, with the hardware already affixed on the back, and lock it into place.

2 | For this kit, these special "moisture mats" sit in the bottom of each pocket. Place one per pocket. They absorb water and slowly return it to the soil.

3 | It's best to plan out your design first. You can experiment by arranging the pots to come up with combinations you like. I thought the rich, dark color of the frame would be a perfect backdrop for a mixture of deep green ferns with highlights of gold and bright green. When you're ready, start planting from the bottom. Remove the ferns from their pots by spreading your pointer and middle fingers apart and placing them over the top of the pot and around the base of the plant. Turn the pot over, and with your other hand gently shake or tap the plant out of its pot. Gently massage and loosen the soil around the top edge, sides, and bottom.

4 | Holding the rootball, set the plant in place. The soil line should be just below the edge of the plastic frame. Check your depth and add soil if necessary.

5 | Add soil as needed to fill in around the rootball. Firm in place with your fingers pointing straight down.

6 | Prepare the next plant, place it in the next compartment, and fill and firm with soil. Continue planting, working your way up.

7 | Finish planting all the planting pockets.

8 | For the finishing touch, tuck in moss, covering any bare soil and open areas. When you're finished, water in each plant. Let the planting lay flat for a couple of weeks, allowing the ferns to get established before hanging on the wall.

The finished project includes *Pellaea rotundifolia*, *Nephrolepis exaltata* 'Tiger', *Microsorum musifolium*, *Pteris cretica* 'Mayii', *Arachniodes simplicior*, and *Asplenium nidus*.

7　**8**

Building a Dish Garden

A dish garden is a grouping of plants that are planted together to create a living arrangement, much as you would design or create harmonious plant combinations outdoors in the garden, only on a much smaller scale. The two most important things to consider in creating a successful dish garden are the plants' cultural requirements and sizes. Because the plants are planted directly into the same container, they experience the same environment. Their roots share the soil, while their above-ground parts receive the same amount of light, temperature, and humidity. For this reason, all the plants must be culturally compatible, enjoying the same growing conditions. It's best to choose plants that won't grow too large for their containers. Otherwise you'll find yourself constantly removing and replacing them, and the planting will always be in a state of flux. Look up information on how big the plants will grow and avoid the common trap of buying young or small versions of much larger plants.

From a design perspective, these miniature landscapes should include at least three different types of plants when you're filling smaller containers, but more varieties can be used with larger containers. Generally, the containers for dish gardens are a good bit wider than they are deep (e.g., bulb pans). This ensures that you'll have room for all your plants without having an excess of soil beneath. While more decorative planters can be used, the planting itself is meant to be the focal point.

Once you have finished planting, feel free to accessorize with natural items or miniatures. Dish gardens can be relatively easy to plant up, which makes them child-friendly. Gather up the family for this fun project.

WHAT YOU'LL NEED

- Planter and saucer. I chose a blue glazed clay container with an attached saucer 8 inches wide × 4 inches (20 × 10 cm) high. Make certain the container has a drainage hole. A plain terracotta bulb pan with the same dimensions also makes a fine container and might be easier to find. You could get even more creative and decorate your terracotta pot if you want to personalize it!

- A piece of window screening. I prefer fiberglass because it is nonreactive and very flexible.

- Scissors.

- Standard fern potting mix, enough to fill the container.

- Three 4-inch (10 cm) potted ferns. The number of plants included, and their pot sizes, will be based on the size of your container. The soil in the pots should be moist. If they are dry, give them a drink, preferably the day before.

- If you prefer to wear gloves, I recommend latex or nitrile gloves. Most other types of gloves are too bulky for small potting jobs.

STEPS

1 | Measure how big a piece of screen you'll need to cover the drainage hole in the planter, leaving some extra to overlap, and cut it. Place the screen over the hole.

2 | Hold the screen in place so it doesn't move and begin filling the container with potting mix. Put in only as much as is needed to reach the bottoms of the rootballs being planted. The end goal is that, when you are finished filling with soil, the soil level at the top will be even with the soil level of the plants being planted. Keep in mind that the final soil line should be approximately ½ inch (13 mm) below the rim, leaving you a watering lip.

3 | Spread your pointer and middle fingers apart and place them over the top of the pot and around the base of the plant. Turn the pot over, and with your other hand gently shake or tap the plant out of its pot. Hint: If you

have rootballs of different sizes, start with the biggest one first. If the rootballs are all the same size, I like to start with the biggest plant first.

4 | Gently massage and loosen the soil around the top edge, sides, and bottom of the rootball. Holding the rootball, set the plant in place. Check your depth and adjust if necessary. Carefully tap out the next plant and loosen the rootball. Set the second plant in place in the container. Again, check the depth and adjust if necessary.

5 | Begin to fill in between and around the ferns with some soil. Firm lightly, with your fingers pointing straight down.

6 | Unpot and prepare the last fern and set it in place. Use your other hand to gently hold back the foliage of the other ferns. Add soil, filling in around the edge and between all the ferns. Then, lightly firm the soil in place, with your fingers pointing straight down.

7 | After all the ferns are planted, I like to give the container a little shake. This will settle, smooth, and even out the soil on the surface. As with any new potting, water your new ferns thoroughly.

The finished arrangement includes *Asplenium antiquum*, *Pteris nipponica*, and *Nephrolepis cordifolia* 'Lemon Buttons'.

Growing a Tabletop Garden

Tabletop gardens offer a creative variation on containerized houseplants. Unlike an arrangement of one or more potted plants on a table or shelf, a tabletop garden unites many plants together to create a complete small-scale garden. There is no limit to what might be adapted for use as a container for a tabletop garden. Look at organizing containers, boxes, or other assorted items with a fresh eye, and use your imagination. Essentially, anything that you can make waterproof and is able to hold plants can become a container for a tabletop garden.

As with vertical gardens, your tabletop garden container can be filled with a potting mix and planted directly, or it can hold individually potted plants. I distinguish tabletop gardens from dish gardens, which are usually smaller, mixed plantings in more typical containers designed with drainage. Tabletop gardens use nontraditional containers—repurposed or custom-built—to create an unconventional, unique look. Tabletop gardens can vary greatly in scale, with larger ones being more "garden-esque."

Tabletop gardens are highly individual and customizable. Unconventional containers require careful preparation, but the results can be well worth the effort. Use or start with a waterproof container so as not to damage furnishings. Carefully adapt a non-waterproof type by lining planting holes or pockets with heavy-duty plastic and sealing all seams or |openings with silicone caulking. Be very careful not to overwater the tabletop garden, since there will not be drainage.

Tabletop gardens are ideal for indoor settings. When used outdoors, they are best treated as temporary or seasonal accents. Establish a theme, and incorporate decorative stones, branches, and miniature accessories to personalize your design. This is a project with no boundaries—let your imagination loose and express your personal style.

WHAT YOU'LL NEED

→ A horizontal container. This one has compartments that can easily hold individual pots. If
you prefer, fill them with potting mix and plant
directly into them. A container that isn't
compartmentalized would best be directly planted.

→ Self-adhesive small bumper pads.

→ Twelve 4-inch (10 cm) potted ferns. The number
of plants used and their pot sizes is based on the
planter you use.

→ Decorative moss. I prefer preserved Spanish moss
for this. Decorative stones, colorful chips, and the
like can also be added to your planting design if
desired.

→ If you prefer to wear gloves, I recommend latex or
nitrile gloves. Most other types of gloves are too
bulky for small potting jobs.

STEPS

1 | Turn the planter over and attach the bumper pads.
Use at least one near every corner. Add more for bigger
containers. The bumpers protect your furnishings by
preventing scratches and allowing for air circulation
underneath the planter.

2 | Lay out your design before you start. Preview
different design options by moving the pots around. I
chose ferns with a blue, silvery, and dark green color
palette to complement the zinc planter. When you're
ready, start by placing the first pot in one corner.

3 | Continue placing pots, one per compartment, until
you've filled them all.

4 | Tuck in moss all around, covering any exposed soil,
bare spots, and pot edges. For more of a miniature
landscape look, you can choose to leave some
compartments unplanted, or planted with smaller
pots and plants. Fill them with stone or colored chips,
creating a "path" or "river" through your garden. Add
miniature figurines and props to complete the look.

The finished project includes *Phlebodium* 'Blue Star',
Davallia mariesii var. *stenolepis*, *Pellaea rotundifolia*,
Pteris ensiformis 'Evergemiensis', and *Platycerium
veitchii* 'Lemoine'.

Crafting Kokedama

Kokedama is a centuries-old Japanese living art form related to bonsai. Translated into English, kokedama means "moss ball." Basically, it is a ball of soil packed around the roots of a plant and then wrapped in moss. Traditionally, kokedama are intended to sit in shallow dishes or be mounted on pieces of driftwood or bark. These days, they are also suspended on strings. A collection of several hanging kokedama make up a Japanese string garden.

Kokedama capture the essence of a pristine environment. Their classic, simple elegance makes for beautiful displays, whether they're resting on tables or shelves, or floating in air. They are also perfect for small spaces.

Ferns are a natural fit, because their variety of textures and forms complement the signature style of kokedama. Additionally, most ferns are not sun dwellers, and because moss balls tend to dry out in direct sun, the ferns will thrive in the more shaded locations for which kokedama are best suited.

Kokedama are absolutely captivating and transformative in any setting and may evoke the reverence for nature that is embraced in Japanese culture. Interestingly, when you're forming the soil ball of kokedama, using both hands is a bilateral activity, which engages both sides of the brain.

WHAT YOU'LL NEED

- Bonsai soil. There are many recipes out there. I used a blend with akadama, lava rock, turface (calcined clay), crushed granite, pumice, charcoal, and vermiculite. All these particles are of small size and suitable for bonsai (see Chapter 3 for more information on soil components and recipes).

- Peat moss, or potting mix consisting mostly of peat moss and a very small amount of fine-grade perlite.

- Mixing bowl.

- Water.

- One 4-inch (10 cm) potted fern. You can also use smaller or larger ferns, but a 4-inch (10 cm) size makes a perfect finished piece!

- Long-fiber sphagnum moss and a bowl of water for soaking.

- Sheet moss and a bowl of water for soaking.

- Cotton string or jute twine. I prefer thin cotton string, but jute works well, too.

- Several feet (a couple meters) of paper-wrapped wire, florist's wire, plastic-coated wire,

monofilament fishing line, or nylon string. Wire cutters. The material must be waterproof so it won't rot. Each material lends its own look. Most of them make for a more natural look, but nylon can also be used to add splashes of color!

- If you prefer to wear gloves, I recommend latex or nitrile gloves. Most other types of gloves are too bulky for small potting jobs.

STEPS

1 | Prepare your kokedama soil. Mix together 1 part bonsai soil and 2 to 2⅓ parts potting mix in a bowl. You'll need about 2 cups (475 ml) for a 4-inch (10 cm) potted fern. Add water, a little at a time, and mix.

2 | When your mix is moist enough, you should be able to form it into a ball.

3 | If you hold the ball with both hands, you should be able to "snap" it in half.

4 | Spread your pointer and middle fingers apart and place them over the top of the pot and around the base of the plant. Turn the pot over, and with your other hand gently shake or tap the plant out of its pot. Gently loosen the rootball and remove some soil, exposing some of the roots without damaging them.

5 | Completely wring out some sphagnum moss as you would a sponge. Wrap the entire rootball with sphagnum moss. Clasp the rootball with both hands and gently squeeze and compress the covered rootball.

6 | Take a long piece of string or twine and tie it tightly around the ball, leaving a short tail on one side and a very long tail on the other side.

7 | Continue wrapping the entire ball, crisscrossing tightly to secure the sphagnum in place, and tie it off with the short tail.

8 | Traditional Japanese technique calls for snapping the soil ball in half, placing the mossed fern inside, and then closing the halves back up. I find this works well with very small rootballs only. For larger rootballs like this one, I find it much easier to build up slowly, packing the soil a little at a time as you work all around.

9 | Once a soil ball has been formed around the roots of the fern, it's time to prepare the materials for covering and hanging your kokedama.

10 | Kokedama can be suspended from one, two, three, or four strings. For the one-string hanging method demonstrated here, first determine how far down you want the kokedama ball to hang. Add an additional 5 to 6 feet (152 to 183 cm) to the length that you want it to hang and cut the piece of paper-coated wire. You can also use a spool of florist's wire, coated wire, monofilament, or nylon string.

11 | Pour the excess water out of the bowl with your sheet moss. Lift the sheet moss pieces out very carefully so as not to break them apart. Squeeze out all the water, again taking care not to twist and tear them. Very carefully "unfold" the layers of sheet moss.

12 | Gently lay sheet moss, green side down, on your work surface. Have several pieces laid out and ready for use. Place the soil ball toward one short side of the moss piece, leaving enough of the sheet moss on the top side to reach over to the center of your ball. Begin wrapping with the moss.

13 | Add more sheet moss as needed, overlapping for complete coverage. Finish by taking a piece to fully cover the bottom. The mossed ball may look lumpy now, but it will flatten out nicely as you tie around it tightly.

14 | Place your wire in the center, on the top, just outside the fern clump. Leave one side the length that you need for the hanger, plus 6 inches (15 cm). The other, longer side will be for wrapping and tying. Holding the wire in place with one finger, take the long end with your other hand and wrap down the side of the moss ball, across the center of the bottom, and back up the opposite side, meeting back at the top. Pulling the wire very tight, twist the two sides together tightly for a few turns to secure it. Coil up the shorter end and tuck it in to keep it out of your way. If you choose to use string instead of wire, tie a couple of knots instead of twisting the wires together.

15 | Now, take the long end and go down one of the other sides, across the bottom center, and back up the opposite side, pulling tightly and holding the tension as you go. Continue wrapping, tying, and crisscrossing until you have secured all around the moss ball. Bring your longer wire back up to the top, and tightly twist it with the shorter end a few times.

16 | Trim the shorter end to 3 inches (8 cm), then tuck it under and wrap it snugly around a section of wire several times to finish off.

The finished project includes *Pteris nipponica*. This one is ready to hang by a single strand.

Variations for Hanging Kokedama

For a 3-strand hanger:

1 | Decide how long you want your hanger to be, and cut three pieces of suitable string that length, plus 4 to 6 inches (10 to 15 cm). Line up the ends and tie a knot at one end.

2 | Place the knot of the hanger on your work surface and spread the three strands apart. Place the center of the moss ball on top of the knot.

3 | Keeping the knot in the center, pull the strands up one at a time, keeping them equally spaced. You can use a florist's greening pin, or even an unfolded paperclip, to pin the knot in the bottom center if it helps. Pull the strings all the way up straight, holding them tightly together, and tie off in a tight knot at the desired length. Trim off any excess over ½ inch (13 mm).

The finished project includes *Nephrolepis cordifolia* 'Jester's Crown'.

To hang your kokedama with four strings, simply follow the same steps as for three strings, except start with four strands. If you don't want a knot at the bottom, another option is to take two long strands, more than double the desired hanging length, line up their ends, and fold in half. Use a small twist tie, florist's greening pin, or unfolded paper clip and secure the folded point in the center, on the bottom of the moss ball. Bring your strings up, equally spaced, pull them straight and taut, hold the loose ends together, and tie a knot.

Two-string hanging is another option, but with the two-string method it's harder to get your kokedama to hang straight. Cut two strings a little longer than the desired hanging length. Tie the first string onto one side of the moss ball, attaching it to several pieces that you tied around the moss. Then tie the second string to the opposite side. Pull them both up straight and taut, so that your kokedama is level, and tie them off in a knot.

Top, left to right: *Nephrolepis cordifolia* 'Jester's Crown', *Pteris nipponica*

Bottom, left to right: *Asplenium antiquum* 'Osaka', *Psilotum nudum*, and *Arachniodes simplicior*

For a monofilament hanger:

Monofilament is not very visible and can make your kokedama appear as if they are floating in air, especially if you use a single string. Take note that monofilament also requires particular knotting practices (see below). Nylon string can provide color. Choose a color to match your décor or make every strand different for a rainbow effect.

Using the three-string method is the easiest for making a monofilament hanger. To tie the strings together at the bottom, use an overhand knot twice.

For a loop at the top of your hanging strands, tie all three together in an overhand knot twice, but cinch them tight while keeping a little loop open. For working with a single string, practice tying an improved clinch knot.

This planting includes *Asplenium antiquum* 'Osaka' and *Arachniodes simplicior*.

MOSS BASKETS, MOUNTS, AND MOSS POLES

The sphagnum moss used in the following three projects grows in bogs. Bogs are wet, acidic, and anaerobic environments. Under these conditions, things decay at an extremely slow rate, and the decaying matter continues to build up in layers over very long periods of time. The deep layers are where peat moss comes from. On occasion, bog bodies have been discovered in peat bogs. One of the oldest is the Haraldskaer Woman from Denmark; she lived around 490 BCE.

Sphagnum moss, living or dead, is very absorptive and extremely acidic, which inhibits the growth of bacteria and fungi. For these reasons, it has been used for centuries as a dressing for wounds, including during World War I. Interestingly, though, along with hay and roses, it can also carry a fungus, *Sporothrix schenckii*. This fungus can cause an infection known as sporotrichosis, sometimes referred to as rose gardener's disease. Most commonly it infects the skin, entering through cuts and abrasions. As a protective measure, I think it's wise to use disposable gloves when working with sphagnum moss. It's also best to wet it before handling it too much to keep the dust down.

Sphagnum peat moss, often simply called peat moss, is a very common soil amendment and a major component of soilless potting mixes. Peat moss is not at all a sustainable crop. Nature cannot regenerate a peat bog at anywhere near the rate at which we are using peat moss. For this reason, we should greatly reduce its use and substitute more renewable resources, such as compost and coir, while continuing to identify other products. The use of peat is not limited to horticulture—it is also used as fuel, among other things. The long-fiber sphagnum used in horticultural projects, such as the projects listed in this book, constitutes a much more limited use of sphagnum. Additionally, it is only the upper portions that are harvested, not the deeper, older layers.

Making Moss Baskets

Moss baskets are both visually and functionally soft, natural ways to hang plants. A variety of ferns are commonly sold as hanging baskets. However, these are typically growing in plastic containers. While some species are comfortable in plastic, many others that grow naturally up in the air will not thrive in plastic containers. Additionally, plastic nursery pots are not as decorative or interesting from an aesthetic standpoint. Moss baskets, however, can be created in a variety of appealing styles.

Keep your eyes open. Anything that has good open drainage and aeration with a sturdy framework can be used for a moss basket. Wire-frame baskets will essentially vanish under the moss, while a wooden framework usually remains more visible. Some more decorative styles are also available; they can combine a distinctive flare with this naturalistic form. Basket frames can be readily found in many shapes and sizes.

Moss baskets are versatile and don't have to be hung. They can also be beautifully displayed sitting on a table or shelf or raised up on a plant stand or pedestal. The latter method is especially suited for ferns with long, dangling fronds. Let your moss basket set off the natural beauty of a favorite fern.

The type of fern you select will determine the type of growing medium to use for this project. For example, epiphytic ferns do not naturally grow in soil and will require a medium closer to their natural environment, such as bark chips. If you're not sure which species of ferns to grow in your moss basket (or in the subsequent two projects) turn to Chapter 3 for a list of good epiphytic ferns for planting in moss baskets, mounting on walls, or establishing moss poles.

WHAT YOU'LL NEED

- I'm using a 10-inch (25 cm) wire basket. Some other options include wooden baskets and terracotta with open designs, available in assorted shapes and sizes.

- Hanger, if desired.

- Long-fiber sphagnum moss and a bowl of water for soaking.

- Well-drained fern potting mix, enough to fill the container at most.

- Four 4-inch (10 cm) potted ferns. The number of plants used and their pot sizes will be based on the size of your container.

- Scissors.

- If you prefer to wear gloves, I recommend latex or nitrile gloves. Most other types of gloves are too bulky for small potting jobs.

STEPS

1 | Completely wring out some sphagnum moss as you would a sponge. Starting at the bottom, begin to line the basket with moss. Make sure the pads of moss are thick enough, and that you overlap them to prevent the soil from falling through.

2 | Because I will be planting three of the ferns into the sides of this basket, I will stop mossing at the level that I want to insert the ferns. Footed ferns, such as these *Davallia*, love creeping over and rooting into moss. Planting into the sides will yield fuller and quicker coverage. The entire basket will be covered with their delicate fronds.

3 | Add some potting mix, staying below the moss line.

4 | Spread your pointer and middle fingers apart and place them over the top of the pot and around the base of the plant. Turn the pot over, and with your other hand, gently shake or tap the plant out of its pot. Gently loosen the rootball, remove a little soil, and compress it with your hands to make it fit through the grid of the basket more easily. Working from the outside, gently push the rootball through an opening in the grid. Rock it back and forth as you push it all the way through, so that the entire rootball is just behind the grid.

5 | Repeat the process with the second fern, using an opening a third of the way around the basket. Repeat for the third fern, going another third of the way around the basket.

6 | Wring out more sphagnum moss, and continue lining the basket all the way up, going over the basket edge a little. Add more potting mix, stopping about ½ inch (13 mm) below the edge. With your fingers pointing straight down, firm the mix around the three rootballs. Next, use your hand to scoop out a hole in the center for the last fern.

7 | Prepare the last fern (but there's no need to compress it) and place it in the hole, making sure that the soil line of the rootball is even with the soil line in the basket (½ inch [13 mm] below the edge). Add soil as needed. Firm in around the rootball of the last plant and give the basket a little shake to smooth and even out the mix. Use scissors to trim the moss and make it neat. Attach the hanger to the basket.

The finished planting includes *Davallia mariesii* var. *stenolepis*.

If you find that your moss baskets dry out too quickly, try this trick. After covering the bottom of the basket's interior with moss, take a shallow saucer, as wide as will fit, and place it in the bottom. Continue filling with mix and plant as usual. You could also use a piece of heavy-duty plastic to line the bottom, but make sure you poke some drainage holes into it first. You can also buy preformed liners, typically made of coir, for standard-sized baskets and just drop them in place. If you want to plant into the sides, cut an "X" into the liner with a sharp knife or scissors, and push the plant through the opening.

Constructing a Fern Mount

Mounts are sometimes referred to as slabs, plaques, or shingles. Many ferns grow happily when mounted to cork slabs, pieces of wood, or actual branches. These sculptural bases lend an architectural dimension to mounted plants. They are often the most natural-looking forms and are also the most natural way for these plants to grow.

Select epiphytic fern species that will feel at home with this method (see Chapter 3 for some good options). Avoid ferns that grow in soil because they will generally dry out too fast, and therefore are not suitable for mounting. Depending on the species you choose, this type of planting may need very regular watering. Be prepared to water as much and as often as is needed. Plunge them into a bucket or give them a little shower and let them drip-dry in your bathroom.

Hang mounted ferns from the ceiling or a wall, singly or in clusters, or simply rest them on a table. Mounts are the perfect way to explore your design prowess and be creative. Mounted displays are anything but ordinary and suggest a feeling of the wild tropics.

WHAT YOU'LL NEED

- Tree round or "cookie," cork slab, or even a piece of plywood.
- Marking pen.
- Drill.
- Hammer and large nail.
- Paper-wrapped wire, plastic-coated wire, or monofilament fishing line. You could also use florist's wire or nylon string.
- Screw eyes or small nails with heads.
- Long-fiber sphagnum moss and a bowl of water for soaking.
- One 6-inch (15 cm) potted fern. The number of plants used and their pot sizes will be based on the piece you are mounting on.

- Wire cutters.
- If you prefer to wear gloves, I recommend latex or nitrile gloves. Most other types of gloves are too bulky for small potting jobs.

STEPS

1 | Look at your tree round and decide what you want to be the top and the front, and where you want to hang the piece from. Mark the location for the hanger.

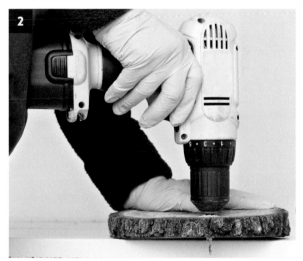

2 | For wood pieces, it is usually easiest to drill the hole. However, you can take a hammer and drive a large nail through the piece if necessary. Always use care with power tools. Drill a hole all the way through, making sure to hold the wood firmly in place, and not to drill through the table.

3 | Put the plastic-coated wire through the hole. Determine how much you want and cut it with the wire cutters. Cross the two ends, leaving at least 1 inch (2.5 cm) on each side, and twist the two together a couple of turns. Then, take one tail and twist it back down on itself tightly, and do the same with the other tail. This is your hanging loop.

4 | Spread your pointer and middle fingers apart and place them over the top of the pot and around the base of the plant. Turn the pot over, and with your other hand gently shake or tap the plant out of its pot. Gently loosen the rootball and remove some soil, exposing some of the roots without damaging them.

5 | Decide the placement and orientation of your fern on the wood. Use your pen to mark the outer edge of the rootball onto the tree round.

6 | Remove the fern, then hammer in some nails around where you made your mark. The nails serve as anchors for your wire.

7 | Completely wring out some sphagnum moss, as you would a sponge. Make a moss pad in the place you've chosen to place your fern.

8 | Cut a piece of paper-coated wire about 6 feet (1.8 m) long. Attach one end of the wire to one of the nails and twist it tightly.

9 | Place the rootball on top of the sphagnum moss. Begin to crisscross the wire, securing the rootball. Wrap it tightly around the nails as you go back and forth.

10 | Once you've basically secured it, twist it tight a few rounds, and leave the long tail in place.

11 | Wring out more moss, and pack it all over and around the rootball. Take the tail and, again, begin crisscrossing over and around the mossed rootball. When it is fully secured, twist it around one of the nails, and then twist it around some of the other wire tightly. Trim it if there's a lot of excess.

The finished project includes *Platycerium bifurcatum*.

FABULOUS CORK

Cork is the outer bark of the cork oak tree, *Quercus suber*. It is native to the Mediterranean region, where it makes up a forest ecosystem. Cork's usage dates back as far as 3000 BCE, when it was used to make corks and to seal vessels. Much of the harvest comes from Portugal, where people have been harvesting cork for 300 years. It is still harvested by hand, a skill passed down through generations.

The cork oak is the only tree that can have its bark removed without killing it. It's harvested every nine years, and the trees have an average lifespan of 200 years. This is a very sustainable practice that keeps the ecosystem going. Cork is naturally waterproof, biodegradable, nontoxic, and totally renewable, making it the perfect base for your mounts! Besides the well-known uses, such as corks for bottles and bulletin boards, cork is used for insulation, sound deadening, flooring, machine-washable clothing and upholstery, and now even 3D printer filament!

Cork also makes a wonderful
mount. Here are two *Asplenium
antiquum* 'Leslie' on a cork piece.

In addition, a simple painted slab of plywood is
another option for mounting ferns. Shown here is
Microsorum musifolium 'Crocodyllus'.

Fashioning a Moss Pole

Moss poles offer another naturalistic way to grow and display your ferns. Structurally, moss poles are formed from wire mesh rolled into a column, stuffed with moss, and planted, much the same way many topiary forms are made. You can get even more creative and make different shapes. Moss poles can be small and delicate or large and robust. They can be planted with a single fern species, in a pattern using several species, or in an informal design.

Epiphytic ferns are perfectly suited to this style (see Chapter 3 for some good options). Some soil-dwelling ferns might be able to adapt to this style, too, as long as you have enough of a moss base or other medium to hold enough water.

This type of planting usually requires very regular watering. Make sure you are prepared to water as much and as often as is needed. Plunge them into a bucket or give them a little shower and let them drip-dry in your bathroom. If you use several different fern species, they should be compatible with each other in terms of the care and conditions they require. Keep in mind that the top of the column will likely dry out faster than the bottom. Take advantage of this and put ferns that are tolerant of less moisture at the top, and those that need the most moisture at the bottom. See the sidebar at the end of this project for a great way to build an internal irrigation system for larger moss poles.

For a fun display, suspend your moss pole from the ceiling or a wall hook. For more variety, try standing one up in a pot. You can even include them in a terrarium. It's easy and fun to make your own collection of moss poles.

WHAT YOU'LL NEED

-» A piece of chicken wire. If you plan to make a larger column, use a heavier wire grid mesh that can hold its own shape and the extra weight. These types of grids also offer bigger planting "holes," so you can usually use 4-inch (10 cm) pots.

-» Measuring tape.

-» Wire cutters.

-» Long-fiber sphagnum moss and a bowl of water for soaking.

-» If you are making a larger column and plan to add some potting mix, have some well-drained fern potting mix available.

-» Twelve 2-inch (5 cm) potted ferns. The number of plants used and their pot sizes will be based on the size of your column.

-» Chopsticks or similar-sized stakes.

-» Scissors.

-» Plastic-coated wire or a ready-made hanger, if desired.

-» If you prefer to wear gloves, I recommend latex or nitrile gloves. Most other types of gloves are too bulky for small potting jobs.

STEPS

1 | Have your design planned out ahead of time. Measure the chicken wire to the desired size. Make sure you allow for an extra row of your grid along the length and at the bottom. These will be needed to secure the column. Use wire cutters to cut to size. Keep the wire pegs on one long side.

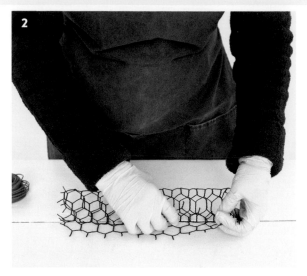

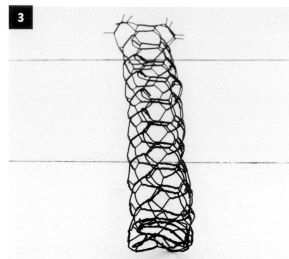

2 | Roll up the chicken wire, leaving the wire pegs at the end. Once rolled, it's time to secure it. Fold the wire pegs over the grid underneath, one at a time, and bend them back to "hook" the mesh closed.

3 | Choose the end with the stronger pegs and close the bottom. Leave the top open.

4 | Completely wring out some sphagnum moss as you would a sponge. Stuff some of the moss into the bottom of the column. This column is 2 inches (5 cm) wide and 10 inches (25 cm) high.

5 | Start planting from the bottom. Take a plant out of its pot and loosen the rootball, removing some of the soil and exposing the roots. Gently squeeze the rootball and push it through the opening in the grid. You can rock it back and forth as you push it in and stretch the grid open a little. Note: If your mesh is too small to fit the rootball through, you can clip the mesh (as little as possible!), put your plant through the hole, and then wire the hole back closed again to keep the plant in place. Make sure the soil line is just behind the wire grid—if you bury the plant it will rot.

6 | Prepare the next fern as you did the first and put it in place. I've chosen four plants each of three types and am planting them in a spiral fashion at even intervals. Wring out more moss, and continue stuffing the column as you go, alternating between a piece of moss and a plant. If you can't fit your fingers in, use the chopstick to tuck moss into all the open spaces. You don't want your roots to dry out.

7 | If necessary, stick the chopstick right down the center of the column to help position the rootballs.

8 | Continue planting and filling with moss. You can add a final plant at the top, or not. Either way, when you are done planting, fold your wire pegs over to close off the top securely.

9 | If you intend to hang it, use a ready-made hanger or decide how big a loop you want. Cut a piece of strong, flexible coated wire, big enough to cross over the top. Make as big a loop as you want and leave at least an extra 1 inch (2.5 cm) on either end. Put one end through the second row of the grid and, taking at least 1 inch (2.5 cm) for a tail, fold it back on itself and twist it tightly all the way up.

10 | Put the other end through the second row of the grid on the opposite side. Keeping your loop the size you want, take at least 1 inch (2.5 cm) for the tail, fold it back on itself, and twist it tightly all the way up. Trim any excess. Now it's ready for hanging.

The finished planting includes *Asplenium antiquum* 'Osaka', *Nephrolepis cordifolia* 'Lemon Buttons', and *Pteris cretica* 'Mayii'.

Variations for Moss Poles

Instead of hanging your moss pole, you can stand it up in a decorative pot. When it's all planted, insert a chopstick, bamboo stake, or metal rod into the bottom of the pole, going up the center. Insert it at least halfway up. The heavier your pole, the stronger your stick needs to be, and the farther up your stick should be inserted. Make sure that enough of the stick remains for it to reach the bottom of the container you will be using.

Place your pole with the stick in the center of a decorative pot and hold it upright, with the stick resting on the bottom of the pot. Fill in with small pebbles, all around, bringing it up to just cover the base of the moss pole and leaving a ¼-inch (6 mm) lip below your pot rim. Your moss pole should be secure. Pebbles or rocks make great filler; you want to give the pot a lot of weight so it doesn't topple over. You could also put some heavy rocks or weights in the bottom of the pot, and if these provide enough ballast, you can fill the rest with whatever you like. Make sure your container has a drainage hole so that excess water can escape.

The finished planting includes *Asplenium antiquum*, *Pteris nipponica*, *Polystichum tsussimense*, and *Nephrolepis exaltata* 'Emina'.

Another variation is to plant your moss pole horizontally, as if it were a log. This can be very handsome! Suspend it from both ends or set it in a long dish. Try your hand at decorative seasonal and holiday plantings, using premade wire forms, such as wreaths, spheres, or trees, or create your own. Fill with moss, and soil if desired, and plant a living wreath for the tabletop or to hang. Ferns display the most beautiful greens, and it's nice to have greenery that is alive and growing! Add decorative touches as you please.

If you are making thicker moss poles, it becomes increasingly harder to soak the medium within. One helpful trick is to cut a piece of PVC pipe the length of your column. Then drill holes all over the pipe, from the top to the very bottom, every few inches. For a narrow column, use a narrower piece of PVC. For a wider column, use PVC with a wider diameter. Seal off the bottom of the pipe with a pipe cap and place this tube in the center of your column as you are building it. Pack your potting medium and/or moss around it. When it's time to water, water the outside and fill up the tube. It will drain out through the holes and water the medium from within.

Creating Fern Prints

Fern prints use living green plants to make art. By pounding on the leaves, you transfer the plant's image onto fabric or paper. These highly desirable, ornamental prints are basically controlled chlorophyll stains—or grown up, glorified grass stains! Make prints on clothing and linens such as towels, table-cloths, and napkins; fabric for various decorative uses; and paper for frame-worthy artwork. They are simply beautiful on their own, but you can easily embellish them further if you desire. Paint them with touches of color, or stitch on some color and texture with additional needlework or beading.

To make a fern print, you'll need to use a very heavy hammer, which makes this a good way to get in a little exercise. And if you've had a bad day, it's a great way to release your tension. You will need a very sturdy surface to work on—such as a basement floor—and should also realize that the process will be very noisy for a few minutes.

Fern prints are very versatile, and every creation is completely unique. Fern printing is a personal favorite of mine.

WHAT YOU'LL NEED

- Heavy wood board (to protect the floor).

- Large, thin sheet of cardboard.

- Canvas fabric or linen napkin for printing.

- Heavy-duty tape. (I chose white duct tape to match the fabric color.)

- Large, sturdy sheet of paper. I use the paper from a large sketch pad.

- Fresh fern fronds.

- Framed canvas.

- Scissors.

- Pencil.

- Heavy lump hammer.

STEPS

1 | Tape the cardboard onto the wooden board. The cardboard provides a smooth surface under the fabric.

2 | Place the area of the linen that you will be printing on the cardboard. Plan your design first. I want to print on the corner of this napkin, so it will be visible even when it's folded. Note: If there are folds or wrinkles in the areas you want to print on, iron them first to smooth the fabric. Put the fern between two pieces of paper towel and blot off all moisture.

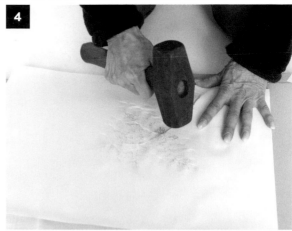

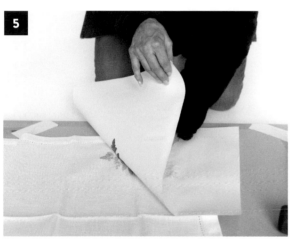

3 | Place your fern where and as you want it. Cover the fern with sturdy, white paper, being careful not to move it. Move the board onto the floor or other suitable surface.

4 | Holding the paper and fabric firmly in place, begin pounding the paper over the fern. Hold the paper as close as possible to the area that you're pounding and be very careful not to hit yourself. If the fern, paper, or fabric shifts, it will blur your design. You might want to practice one first. Pound as hard as you repeatedly in one spot before continuing along. Work in one direction, moving from one end to the other.

5 | Once you have completely pounded the whole fern, very gently and slowly begin to peel back the paper. If the design didn't transfer, you may need to cover it up again and pound some more.

6 | See the print on the napkin and on the paper! The paper is beautiful in its own right and could be framed as art as well.

TO MAKE A HANGING CANVAS

1 | Place the framed canvas on the canvas fabric to be printed. Be sure to have the right side of the fabric facing up. Measure out how much you will need to cover the entire front and a border all the way around that you will tape in back when done. Cut your fabric to size.

2 | With the frame still centered on the canvas fabric, pencil a line all the way around to mark the boundary for your design. Now, take the fabric, create your design with some fronds (working within the pencil-line boundary), and make your print following the steps outlined on the previous page.

3 | Line the printed fabric up on the frame.

4 | Fold one edge over and tape the corners in back. Repeat on the opposite edge.

5 | Cover your work surface with clean paper or toweling and place the print face down. Tape the entire length of both edges. This keeps the print flat and secure and prevents the fabric from fraying. It also looks nicer.

6 | Now fold in the remaining edges and wrap it like a present. To make it less bulky, cut the little flap of fabric on top where it meets the tape at the edge of the frame, and remove it. Tape the entire length to the edge of the frame.

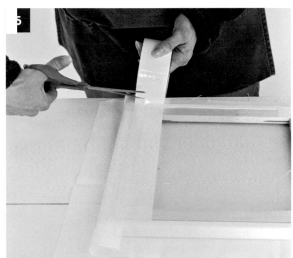

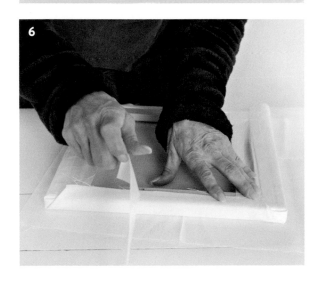

Making Pressed Fern Art

Botanists have been pressing plants since the 1500s. By collecting pieces of plants, pressing them flat, and drying them, you can preserve them. Mounted on paper and intended for study, these botanical specimens are often quite attractive. Their beauty didn't go unnoticed in Victorian England. It was quite fashionable for ladies to collect and press plants in order to create picturesque albums for viewing pleasure. Today, the pressing technique is basically unchanged, and creating artistic specimens for decoration is increasingly popular.

Although dried and pressed ferns may no longer be alive, they are still the real deal and lend a truly naturalistic element to artwork. Make pictures for hanging, create notecards, or start a keepsake album. Their look complements any style of décor. If you like the idea of working with pressed plants but want even more creative freedom, try a variation of this theme: clipped pressed art. Instead of using your dried pressed specimens in whole pieces, you can clip them into smaller segments and recombine the pieces to create all kinds of artful designs.

You can make pressed art of any size. It is a quick, easy, inexpensive decorating fix, and it makes a great gift, too!

WHAT YOU'LL NEED

- Pruning shears.
- Fern fronds.
- Paper towels.
- Several sheets of newspaper.
- A big, heavy book. You can also buy or make your own plant press.
- Sturdy paper for your finished design.
- Mat for framing, if desired.
- Frame.
- Ruler.
- Pencil.
- Scissors.
- Scrap paper for working on.
- Flat knife.

- White glue.
- Pointed toothpicks.
- Paper towel or napkin.
- Heavy washers for weights.

STEPS

1 | Harvest your fronds using pruning shears. Place your fronds between paper towels, and blot completely dry. Place dried fronds on one side of the newspaper, fold over, and cover with the other side. Place a heavy book on top. Let the fronds press and dry for a minimum of 24 hours—I often wait a week.

2 | Measure and cut your final mounting paper to fit inside the frame. If using a mat, cut the paper to the outside dimensions of the mat. Trim away any excess.

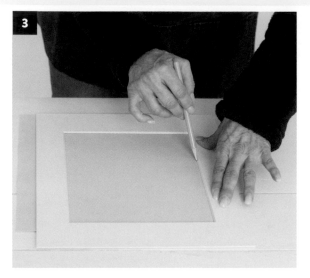

3 | Mark the inside of the mat (or the frame if you're not using a mat) so you know the boundary for your design.

4 | Carefully remove the dried specimens from the newspaper and create your design. You might want to play with it on a piece of scrap paper first, so as not to ruin your mounting sheet. When you're ready, use a pencil to lightly mark the placement of your fronds.

5 | Slide the knife gently under the first frond and lift it up (for a complex design, start with the biggest frond first). Carefully turn it over onto a piece of scrap paper. Gently apply the tiniest drops of glue. You might want to practice some of these techniques before you do your final design.

6 | Use a toothpick to spread the glue even thinner. Then, use the knife to lift the frond from the paper.

7 | Gently turn the frond over, taking care not to touch the glue. Place the bottom on its mark and hold gently with one finger. Pivot the top of the frond over to its mark and put it in place.

8 | Place a paper towel over the frond and press down gently but firmly. If necessary, wrap a napkin tightly around your pointer finger and carefully dab up any excess glue from the paper.

9 | Place weights all over the frond to hold it in place while the glue dries.

10 | It should be dry in a day. Once it's dry, carefully remove the weights. Remove the back from the frame, place the mat inside if you're using one, place your pressed art inside, and close the frame. Your artwork is ready for display.

Instead of mounting your pressed ferns in a permanent display, simply place them temporarily on a desk blotter, paper, or even fabric. Splatter or brush paint all over and around them to create cool fern silhouettes. Another option is to find a recipe for making your own paper, and then for added beauty and interest, add bits of fern leaves to the mix.

Clipped Pressed Art

Create clipped art using all the techniques described above. Take your dried fronds and clip them into smaller pieces. Assemble them, creating your own unique design.

Making Cyanotypes

A cyanotype, one of the oldest "photographic" techniques, is a photochemical blueprinting. It was first discovered in 1842 by Sir John Herschel, an English scientist, who used the method mainly to produce copies of diagrams. These were the original blueprints.

The process is based on a chemical's sensitivity to ultraviolet light. After a piece of paper or fabric is coated with a solution of the chemical, it is then exposed to sunlight, which includes ultraviolet light. The light reacts with the chemical, and a complex chemical reaction follows, resulting in an insoluble blue dye called Prussian blue. Any part of the paper or fabric that is covered before being exposed to the light will remain white (or whatever the original color of the paper or fabric was). Any part that is exposed turns blue.

Anna Atkins (1799–1871) was an English botanist and is often considered the first female photographer. She is very well known for her work with cyanotypes. Anna used this process to document plant life, most notably ferns, algae, and seaweed. After treating the paper with the chemical solution, she would place the specimens directly onto the coated paper and expose it to sunlight. She produced a series of impressive books filled with these blue Victorian photograms. Cyanotypes are also a bit reminiscent of Matisse's blue paintings, especially those with plantlike images.

Nowadays you might hear of cyanotypes being called sunprints. A variety of kits and a wide assortment of pretreated paper and fabric in many colors are readily available. If you are more adventurous, you can still obtain the same chemicals and treat your own paper or fabric. Make clothing, linens, decorative artwork for display, notecards, and much more. This is an easy and exciting project for children, and fun for the whole family.

- Paper towels.
- Fern fronds.
- Plain scrap paper.
- A sturdy, lightweight board. I use foam board.
- Pretreated papers and/or napkins in lightproof bags.
- Heavy black paper, cloth, or plastic.
- Plexiglas or glass sheet.
- Sturdy, flat piece of corrugated cardboard.
- A sunny day.
- A sink or bathtub for rinsing.

STEPS

1 | Blot the fern fronds dry with paper towels. Do a mock-up of your designs on plain paper. Ready everything you plan to make in advance. You cannot expose the treated materials to light for very long. Try to avoid working in a sunny, bright room. Because the fern fronds are only creating a silhouette here, they don't have to be fresh and green. If you press them for a day or so, it will make them nice and flat and easy to work with, and they will create sharper images.

2 | If you are doing more than one cyanotype project at a time, place them on your foam board to make sure they will all fit.

3 | Have the lightproof bags with pretreated materials on hand. Remove the treated paper from the bag and swap it out for the plain paper. This notecard is actually light blue paper but looks dark blue because of the chemical coating.

4 | Immediately cover with the lightproof package to block out light. You can also use heavy, black paper for covering.

1

5 | Remove the next piece of treated paper from its bag and swap it out for the plain paper. Be careful not to mess up your design. This sheet is white paper but looks blue due to the chemical coating. Transfer your design to the treated sheet. When done, immediately cover with the lightproof package to block out light.

6 | If you're making a napkin instead of paper, remove the treated napkin from its bag and open it completely on the foam board. Place your design. This napkin is white but appears blue due to the chemical coating.

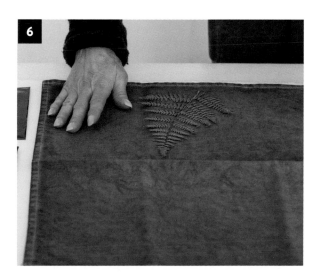

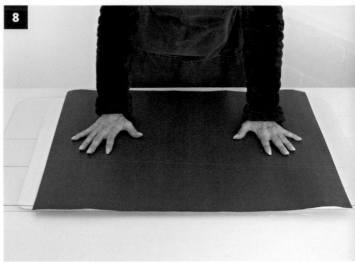

7 | As soon as the last piece is ready, carefully remove the black pouches and cover the entire board with a sheet of plexiglas (glass works perfectly, too). Set it down carefully so as not to move any of the fronds. Take care not to get smudges on the plexiglas.

8 | Immediately cover with a piece of heavy, black paper. A heavy, black cloth or thick black plastic will also work.

9 | Carefully place the foam board onto a piece of corrugated cardboard. This makes it easier to move around. Carry it outside and place it in a flat spot in direct sunlight. From noon to early afternoon is the best time of day. Remove the black paper and leave it in the sun for 20 to 30 minutes. Stay with it to make sure that nothing disturbs it or falls on it. Remove anything that lands on the plexiglas, and make sure no shadows fall on it.

10 | Bring everything inside exactly as it is. At this point, you have only printed one side of your pieces. If you want to print on both sides, a napkin for example, turn the piece over and repeat the entire process right away. Even if you don't want to make a design, the backside of the piece will ultimately be the original color. For example, the napkin will be white on the back. If you want it to be the same blue as the front, you must expose the back to sunlight for the same amount of time. When you are done exposing your pieces, begin rinsing them in the sink, one at a time. Handle paper gently and try not to rub it.

11 | Notice the transformation of the coloring! When you are finished rinsing, lay the paper flat to dry.

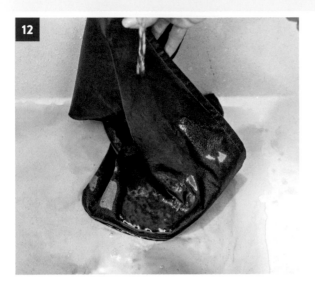

12 | For the napkin, run it under water, watching all the chemicals rinsing out.

13 | When you are done rinsing the napkin, wring the excess water out of the fabric, shake it out, and lay it flat to dry.

14 | The dark blue napkin was exposed to 30 minutes of strong midday sun, hence the strong coloration. The medium blue napkin didn't get any direct sun, and it was at the very end of the day. The less you expose your item to sunlight, the lighter blue it will be. You decide.

By buying papers treated with different colors, you can create beautiful, colored notecards or fun pieces to frame.

About the Author

MOBEE WEINSTEIN is the foreman of gardeners for outdoor gardens at the New York Botanical Garden (NYBG) in the Bronx. She has a degree in plant studies and has done postgraduate work in botany. She taught indoor plants as an adjunct professor at the State University of New York (SUNY) and is a regular instructor at the New York Botanical Garden. She has appeared representing the NYBG on television (NBC, ABC, *Martha Stewart Living*, and others) and radio (Ralph Snodsmith's *The Garden Hotline* program and more). She is a frequent lecturer to outside organizations and a judge for the Philadelphia Flower Show (ferns and other plant classes). She has also judged the NYC Community Gardens and organized and led field trips for the NYBG School of Professional Horticulture. She has published more than a dozen articles and book chapters on various topics, including ferns and water lilies.

Photo Credits

ALAMY: PAGES 20, 90, 92, 94, 95, 100, 105, 107, 109, 118, 120, 149, 151, 155, 158, 174, 175

CHRISTINA BOHN PHOTOGRAPHY: PAGES 6, 42, 43, 45, 46, 47, 48, 52, 54, 60, 61, 67, 69, 70, 76, 88 (RIGHT), 176, 178, 179, 180, 181, 182, 183, 184, 185, 186, 187, 188, 189, 190, 191, 192, 193, 194, 195, 196, 197, 198, 199, 200, 201, 202, 203, 204, 205, 206, 207, 208, 210, 211, 212, 213, 214, 215, 216, 217, 218, 219, 220, 221, 222, 223, 224, 225, 226, 227, 228, 229, 230, 231, 232, 233, 234, 235, 236, 237, 238, 239, 240, 241, 242, 243, 244

WENDY CUTLER: PAGE 102

GETTY IMAGES/JERRY PAVIA: PAGE 148

GLENN SCOTT PHOTOGRAPHY: PAGE 72

HOLLY NEEL ILLUSTRATION: PAGES 32 (BOTTOM), 39

ISTOCK: PAGES 89, 121, 123

MILETTE GARDEN PICTURES: PAGES 104, 143, 168

NORTH CREEK NURSERIES (WWW.NORTHCREEKNURSERIES): PAGE 165

PLANT DELIGHTS NURSERY, INC (WWW.PLANTDELIGHTS.COM): PAGE 119, 167, 173

PLANT SYSTEMATICS: PAGES 2, 3, 96, 106, 110, 112, 113, 115, 150

SHUTTERSTOCK: PAGES 8, 9, 10, 11, 12, 15, 17, 18, 21, 22, 24, 26, 28, 30, 32 (TOP), 33, 34, 35, 37, 40, 41, 49, 50, 56, 58, 63, 65, 72, 74, 75, 77, 78, 80, 81, 85, 86, 88 (LEFT), 91, 93, 97, 98, 99, 101, 102, 103, 111, 116, 117, 122, 124, 126, 129, 130, 133, 134, 136, 137, 138, 139, 141, 142, 144, 145, 146, 147, 152, 153, 154, 157, 159, 160, 161, 162, 163, 164, 165, 166, 169, 170, 171, 172, 248

VITROPLUS: PAGE 108, 114

Index

X